JOHN BAILEY'S FISHING GUIDES

WHERE TO
FLY
FISH
IN BRITAIN
& IRELAND

JOHN BAILEY'S FISHING GUIDES

WHERE TO
FLY
F SH
IN BRITAIN
& IRELAND

John Bailey

NEW HOLLAND

This edition published in 2006 by New Holland Publishers (UK) Ltd
London   Cape Town   Sydney   Auckland

2 4 6 8 10 9 7 5 3 1

www.newhollandpublishers.com

First published in 2002 by New Holland Publishers (UK) Ltd

Garfield House, 86–88 Edgware Road, London W2 2EA
80 McKenzie Street, Cape Town 8001, South Africa
14 Aquatic Drive, Frenchs Forest, NSW 2086, Australia
218 Lake Road, Northcote, Auckland, New Zealand

ISBN 1 84537 309 X

Edited and designed by Design Revolution Limited,
Queens Park Villa, 30 West Drive, Brighton BN2 2GE
Project Editor: Ian Whitelaw
Designer: Lindsey Johns
Editor: Julie Whitaker

Index by Indexing Specialists,
202 Church Road, Hove BN3 2DJ

Series Editor: Kate Michell
Assistant Editor: Kate Parker
Editorial Assistant: Anne Konopelski
Publishing Manager: Jo Hemmings
Production Controller: Joan Woodroffe

Reproduction by Pica Digital Pte Ltd, Singapore
Printed and bound in Singapore by Kyodo Printing Co (Singapore) Pte Ltd

CONTENTS

INTRODUCTION

Let me say from the outset that this is not a comprehensive guide to all the game fishing in Britain and Ireland. There is simply not enough space for me to do that. Rather, I'm trying to point you in the right direction so that you can find some appealing fishing wherever you may be. I like to imagine this book in the cubby hole of your car – always handy, always there to give you a good idea or two, and a bit of inspiration.

In many ways, this book has been a labour of love; either I found myself enjoying some spectacular fishing or I've been on the phone for two or three hours talking to pals around the country. Work doesn't come better than that! It's certainly great to hear people talk about the waters they love with enthusiasm.

The great thing about fly fishing is its simplicity. A rod, a reel, a few flies, Polaroid glasses, Wellingtons and you're off. You can pop your outfit in the car boot and travel to any point of the compass, knowing that if you find yourself near a water with a few hours on your hands, then you're ready to go. Two hours or eight hours, it doesn't really make a lot of difference. Unlike coarse fishing, you don't need to prepare bait, feed up a swim or anything like that... no, once the fly is on the tippet and in the water, you stand a good chance of a fish, and that can be within two minutes of leaving the car park.

It's for this reason, I believe, that fly fishing is one of the few growth areas in angling in this country today. It fits nicely into a hectic lifestyle. If you're on holiday with the family and want to give them the bulk of your time, you can still sneak out for a couple of hours on your own. If you're a business-man who finishes a meeting early, then there might be something for you before dinner. More and more retired couples are coming to the sport, so why not take this book and a couple of rods, head off into the great wide beyond and find some perfect places to fish?

I don't know what particular branch of game fishing you're into, but hopefully there will be plenty for you in the book. I've covered all parts of the country and all types of fishing, from commercial ponds outside London to deserted moorland lochs. You'll find waters for salmon, sea trout, wild brown trout, stocked rainbows, grayling and even the odd mullet and bass. So, whether you're urban or rural, north or south, still water or river, there will be an entry that makes the nerves tingle!

This has been a very interesting book for me to write. It's reinforced for me just what a huge amount of fishing we have without going abroad for more. It's tempting to dash off to the Kola or Alaska or wherever, but in fact we've got some cracking places that don't require any air miles. In fact, in all probability, we've got more trout fishing now than at any time in the last twenty years: rivers are getting cleaner, and commercial fisheries are now providing a really satisfactory product. Once upon a time, it was enough to dig a puddle, throw in a few stumpy-finned rainbows, and the punters would come running. Not now. We've grown more sophisticated, and unless commercial fisheries cater accordingly, they'll go bust.

I've also learned how important it is to ask advice at any fishery you visit. It's often a little intimidating when you first go to a new water. Where do you begin? What sort of fly, at what sort of level? And so on, and so on. Yet every water mentioned in this book will give free and generous advice. Of course, it's in the best interests of the fishery owners to see you go away happy and successful. There's nothing to be ashamed of if you're primarily a still-water man and you're visiting a river for the first time. You'll need a bit of guidance, and never forget that with confidence comes success.

I've become aware that catch and release is now a major part of the game fishing scene. For salmon, in many places, it's just about compulsory. The feeling is that wild salmon are just too precious to think of killing. Research has proven that the vast majority of salmon caught, unhooked and returned will plough on upstream to fulfil their spawning instincts. Certainly, while salmon are in such short supply around our shores, it's good sense to think of the future and return those fish. Any wild fish, come to that. Do we actually need to take wild browns home with us? I doubt it. Even when it comes to specifically stocked rainbows, the feeling is increasingly to let the better fish go back. Who wants to eat a five-pound rainbow anyway? No, take what you want to eat or give away, and put the rest back.

I've also learned that imitative patterns are holding ever-greater sway in the fly-fishing world. Go back twenty years and, on most commercial fisheries at least, you would find the vast majority of anglers stripping back lures as though their lives depended on it. Of course, lure fishing has a very valid place in fishing, but it's not the be all and end all. Many fisheries are actively encouraging anglers to use smaller and smaller flies and to fish them more thoughtfully. This is good for the fisherman and it certainly helps the fish stocks.

Angling is increasingly blending into the general countryside scene. Anglers on the big Midland reservoirs, for example, are expected to co-operate with birdwatchers, walkers and yachtsmen. We're all there enjoying a natural resource together, and it's important that a spirit of goodwill exists between all the groups involved. We are a well-mannered lot, we fishermen, but do remember that voices carry across water, especially when it's calm or at dusk, so no matter how frustrating it is to lose that last fish, let's keep our frustrations to ourselves!

In these pages, you'll find some of my favourite fishing waters. Hopefully, this book will have an impact on you too and, chances are, some day in the near future we'll meet up, perhaps share a reminiscence and, who knows, you might be able to put me onto the right fly for the day. Tight lines.

Scale

mls 0 10 20 30 40 50 60 70 80 90 100
kms 0   20   40   60   80   100

SCOTLAND

GLASGOW   EDINBURGH

LONDONDERRY

BELFAST

NEWCASTLE UPON TYNE
SUNDERLAND

IRELAND

THE NORTH

DUBLIN

BRADFORD   LEEDS   HULL

MANCHESTER
LIVERPOOL
SHEFFIELD

LIMERICK

STOKE-ON-
TRENT   DERBY   NOTTINGHAM

WATERFORD

LEICESTER

WOLVERHAMPTON

CORK

BIRMINGHAM   COVENTRY

EAST
ANGLIA

THE
MIDLANDS

WALES

CARDIFF   BRISTOL

LONDON

SOUTH
WEST

THE
SOUTH

SOUTH
EAST

SOUTHAMPTON

N

PLYMOUTH

FLY-FISHING SITES IN THE SOUTH WEST

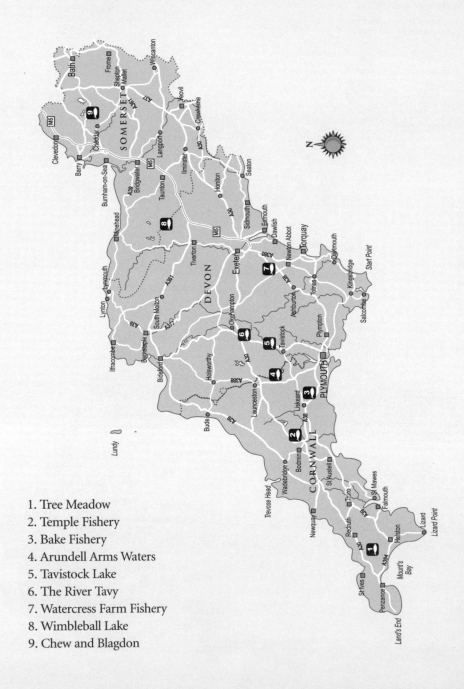

1. Tree Meadow
2. Temple Fishery
3. Bake Fishery
4. Arundell Arms Waters
5. Tavistock Lake
6. The River Tavy
7. Watercress Farm Fishery
8. Wimbleball Lake
9. Chew and Blagdon

*' The rivers of the West Country are unique. There are over
sixty of them in the three counties of Somerset, Devon and
Cornwall, running down from the great uplands of Exmoor,
Dartmoor and Bodmin – wild unspoilt rivers that the French
would call "primitif". All of them hold abundant brown
trout, and many have big runs of salmon and sea trout. This
is a part of England where kingfishers and buzzards still fly,
where you can fish all day and see no-one, where the rivers
are still clean and full of life and sparkle. '*

ANNE VOSS BARK, OWNER OF THE ARUNDELL ARMS AND REVERED FLY FISHER

A nne is quite right. There is something uniquely special
about fly fishing in the West Country on rivers that dance
along, simply singing out to you, 'Fish me, fish me, please'. It
sometimes seems that every valley is gushing with water,
generally crystal clear, and frequently full of fish. Perhaps the
sea trout runs – 'peal' as they call them in these parts – aren't
quite what they once were, but there are still fish aplenty, and in
surroundings that you'll never forget.

But there's more. Anybody who has fished Chew, Blagdon or
the heart-stoppingly beautiful Wimbleball can tell you that.
Wimbleball is probably my personal favourite, nestling in the
most beautiful countryside. The West Country is fortunate in
having some top-class commercial fisheries; the standard, in my
view, is probably higher than in any other part of the country.
So there really is something here for everybody. What's more, if
you fancy it and you're up to it, there's even fly fishing around
the coast for the king of the inshore waters, the bass.

The South West is a holiday paradise for the whole family.
There are beautiful beaches and rugged coves, quaint villages
and thriving market towns. You can explore the moors, walk
the coastal paths or visit old properties and exciting gardens.
But, above all, don't forget to bring that fishing rod!

THE SOUTH WEST

TREE MEADOW – CORNWALL

I'll never forget my first – and, it has to be said, only – visit to Tree Meadow. The water is just beautiful, the fish are spectacular and the fishing itself is so thrilling, it's an expedition I'll never forget. Tree Meadow is a stunning place, surrounded by woods and fields, and you're so far south-west that you really can believe you're in another world. Certainly, it's a world that grips you totally since the fish are big, the water is clear and the whole experience is utterly fascinating. Tree Meadow comprises the larger Willow Lake and the smaller Sedge Lake, and they're both fabulously rich in natural food stocks – one of the things that accounts for both the browns and the rainbows being in such excellent condition.

There are some very large fish around, and double-figure rainbows are not rare, so don't consider using leaders less than five pounds in weight. This is very much a stalking water, so don't forget your peaked cap and your Polaroids and all the usual imitative patterns. Dry fly often works – try hawthorn, black gnat, sedges, daddies and so on. Buzzers, too, work very well indeed, and if you don't see fish moving on the surface, damsels, corixa, shrimps and beetles will all catch their fair share of fish. Nowhere are the lakes much over twelve to fifteen feet in depth, so the chances are that a

❧ CATCH AND RELEASE ❧

Catch and release is rightfully a growing trend. However, there is no point releasing a fish that is condemned to die a slow, lingering death because of bad handling. To avoid harming a fish, follow these rules:
- *Always fish with barbless hooks for easy release.*
- *Try to avoid taking a fish from the water at all if you possibly can. Unhook it in the margins.*
- *Never touch a fish with dry hands.*
- *Play a fish quickly and firmly – though not ruthlessly – so it is not exhausted in the battle.*
- *Never use unnecessarily light leaders as this simply prolongs the fight and increases the chance of a break-off.*
- *Always carry forceps with you for quick and easy unhooking.*
- *Hold the fish upright, into a current if possible, until it is strong enough to swim away. A fish that sinks to the bottom on its back will drown.*
- *If a fish is deep hooked and appears to be bleeding, in all probability it's best to kill it as quickly and cleanly as possible.*

floating line is pretty much the only thing you'll need, though at times, in very hot weather, it does pay to put on a long leader and get down deep.

You're pretty well assured of a lovely day's fishing at Tree Meadow in beautiful surroundings, and a very warm and generous welcome.

☀ SEASON – open all year.

⚡ TICKETS – phone 01736 850899 or write to Tree Meadow, Deveral Road, Fraddam, Hayle, Cornwall. On Willow Lake, a day ticket costs £35 for four fish and £21 for two fish. You can practise catch and release on Sedge Lake for a £20 day ticket or an evening ticket of £15.

⚖ RECORDS – rainbows 17lb 8oz and browns 10lb 7oz.

➡ DIRECTIONS – leave the A30 for Hayle and drive through the town until you come to a mini-roundabout before a viaduct. Take the first left off this roundabout onto the B3302. You will reach Fraddam village. Take the next left, signposted Deveral Road. Tree Meadow Fishery is about a mile on the right.

🛏 ACCOMMODATION – phone the Tourist Information Centre at St Ives on 01736 796297 for information on accommodation in the area.

TEMPLE FISHERY – CORNWALL

Temple Fishery is beautifully situated, especially Mallard Lake, an old china clay pit that has matured totally and now blends seamlessly into the landscape of Bodmin Moor. There are now two lakes in the fishery. Mallard has an area of almost three acres and is up to forty feet deep with a twenty-five-foot average. Teal Lake is larger, at four and a half acres, but shallower. The deepest holes there are fifteen feet, with an average of eight feet.

Both waters are very well cared for, but the abundant vegetation really does foster a feeling of privacy. The waters are largely spring-fed but this doesn't stop them having a slightly peaty tinge to them – remember that they are dug into the bowels of the moor itself. They're both rich lakes and this probably explains why the owner, Julian Jones, recommends damsel nymphs and especially buzzers, of which the lakes have big hatches. Also, over the last couple of years, mayfly have been seen in increasing numbers and there's every chance of a really significant hatch in the near future.

Obviously, the two different lakes can demand different approaches – especially on really bright, hot days when the fish have the ability to get down really deep in Mallard Lake. It's then that a fast-sinking line really comes into its own with perhaps a larger fly such as the Montana or a Woolly Bugger. The best strategy is to retrieve very slowly and to give the fish plenty of time to see what's going on. One last tip – Bodmin is no stranger to gusty winds, and this often produces a build-up of terrestrials. At the right times of the year, daddy patterns work exceedingly well.

☀ SEASON – open all year.

✦ TICKETS – phone Julian on 01208 821730 for prior booking or write to Temple Trout Fishery, Temple Road, Bodmin, Cornwall. On both Teal Lake and Mallard, a five-fish limit costs £24. However, the stocked fish are smaller on Teal Lake than on Mallard – averaging just a pound or so. On Mallard, the stocked fish average one and a half to two pounds with some very big fish present. A sporting ticket costs £13.

➡ DIRECTIONS – if you're travelling west across Bodmin Moor on the A30, Temple Fishery is about four miles past the Jamaica Inn on the left side of the road. It is very well signposted.

⊨ ACCOMMODATION – Bodmin is close by and both the north and south Cornish coasts are easily accessible. Phone the Tourist Information Centre in Bodmin on 01208 76616 for further details.

BAKE FISHERY – CORNWALL

Right down in Cornwall you'll find the excellently run Bake Fishery, which has three trout lakes set in lovely, rolling countryside. In all, there are about eight acres of water to be fished, but the great thing is that under nearly all conditions you'll find fish on or near the surface, so chances are that all you'll need is a floating line, a selection of dry flies (black gnats and grey dusters are favourites), some buzzers, emergers, goldheads and nymphs. Yes, this is exciting hands-on fishing. The rainbows themselves are exciting, too: the hallmarks of a Bake fish are a full set of fins and a rainbow that really powers off. My own advice is to purchase one of the 'rover' tickets, as this allows you to move around freely, swapping from one lake to another and really exploring everything the fishery has to offer.

There is some catch and release allowed – something I'm very much in favour of. It allows fish to mature and also to develop a cunning that makes them a very serious challenge to the angler indeed. You're just beginning to think that the fish in front of you have seen it all before when suddenly your buzzer is taken, your line zaps a couple of inches forwards and you're playing a fish that really and truly does have you with your heart in your mouth. The fishing here really is excellent, and Bake is highly recommended.

☀ SEASON – open all year.

✦ TICKETS – contact Tony Lister on 01752 849027 at Bake Fishing Lakes, Trerulefoot, Nr. Saltash, Cornwall, PL12 5BL. There is a whole range of ticket prices but, as an example, a five-fish limit costs £25 and a four-fish limit £22. You can also catch and release for £10 a day.

⚑ RECORDS – the rainbow record is nearly 12lb 8oz and the brown record is just into double figures.

⚏ FACILITIES – tackle hire is available, along with some tuition. There are toilets on site and disabled facilities.

➜ **DIRECTIONS** – a few miles before Liskeard on the A38 take the Bake exit on the Trerulefoot roundabout. Take the first right, then the first left and after about a quarter of a mile you will find the fishery entrance on the right-hand side .

⊨ **ACCOMMODATION** – the coastal towns of Fowey and Looe are close, as is the county town of Plymouth. Phone the Tourist Information Centre in Plymouth on 01752 304849 for details.

ARUNDELL ARMS WATERS – DEVON

If you're touring the South West you really owe it to yourself to pop into the Arundell Arms for a couple of days – or more if you've got the time and the money. The reason is simple: you just won't find better, more beautiful, more superbly managed river fishing anywhere in the country. The few days that I've spent at the Arundell Arms over the years have remained highlights in my fishing life – every single solitary one of them. I don't know if it's the countryside, the rivers or the friendly, helpful efficiency of the hotel's ghillies, but I've never left without aching to return.

The charm of the Arundell rivers is that they're wild. The Lyd, the Wolf, the Carey and the tiny Thrushel all rise on Dartmoor and bring the wildness of that bleak area down into the valleys. These are flashing, chattering rivers. Shallow and clear, often overgrown – they offer a huge challenge, and the hours melt by. The trout aren't generally large, but they're as wild as leopards and on light gear – which is obligatory – they fight like leopards, too.

All these rivers join their more serious parent, the Tamar, within a mile of the hotel and this is where the serious salmon fishing begins. The average weight is around ten pounds but twenty-pounders are caught.

We haven't even looked at the sea trout fishing yet, which can be excellent on the Tamar, Lyd and Thrushel. In fact, my first real sea trout fishing took place on the Lyd. A mild, high summer evening. A moon masked by light cloud. A pool full of fish. A large artificial skating the surface near the tail. A rise. A tug. A screaming reel and a memory that lives on brightly.

SEASON – the trout fishing opens on 15 March and closes on 30 September. Sea trout fishing opens on 3 March – even though fish don't really arrive until June – and closes on 30th September. Salmon fishing opens on 1 March – although mid April is the earliest fish can arrive in normal conditions – and closes on 14 October. The very best brown trout fishing is in May, June and September. Sea trout fishing is at its best in July and August and the salmon fishing builds up to a crescendo, peaking in September and October.

RULES – the hotel operates a system of beat rotation. In order to preserve wild stocks, the hotel asks that no more than one salmon, four sea trout and four brown trout are kept during any twenty-four hour period. Barbless hooks are encouraged for safe return of fish.

⊨ **TICKETS AND ACCOMMODATION** – these are all available from the Arundell Arms,

Lifton, Devon PL16 0AA, which can be reached on 01566 784666.

→ DIRECTIONS – Lifton can be found just off the A30 between Okehampton and Launceston. The Arundell Arms is on the High Street of this very pretty, now by-passed, village. The fishing is all within easy access.

TAVISTOCK LAKE – DEVON

Tavistock Lake is another of these wonderfully run, sublimely attractive commercial fisheries that have developed recently. It consists of three lakes – Kingfisher Lake and Heron Lake, which are stocked more routinely, and Osprey Lake, which contains some really outsized fish and offers that much more of a challenge. The size of the rainbows in the two former lakes averages around the two-pound mark, whereas in Osprey things kick-off at three pounds and above... going all the way up to the fishery record of thirty pounds – a one-time rainbow record a few years ago.

But it's not necessarily the size of the fish that makes a fishery, and Tavistock is beloved by the regulars for far more than pounds and ounces. The lakes are pretty, the stocking levels are good, the atmosphere is warm and generous and the fishing is all you'd want. The lakes are rich – there are even nice mayfly hatches – and respond to imitative patterns. You can, of course, take fish on lures, but look first to nymphs, buzzers and dry flies.

Osprey is considered the hardest lake of all and it offers a real challenge in its moody, fascinating way. But that's the delight of fishing, isn't it? And believe me, once banked, those rainbows are worth every minute of effort. So if it's a well-tended, verdant venue you're looking for, Tavistock is for you.

SEASON – open all year.

TICKETS – contact Abigail Underhill at Tavistock Lake, Parkwood Road, Tavistock, Devon, PL19 9JW on 01822 615441. For Osprey Lake, a five-fish limit costs £44 and a two-fish limit, £21. There's a range of ticket prices in between. For Kingfisher and Heron Lakes, the five-fish limit costs £23. You'll need an environment agency (rod) licence. This is available from most post offices and costs £23.50 for a year. A junior licence is £5 a year and disabled and OAP concessions £11.75. An eight-day licence is £8.25 and a one-day licence £3.

RECORDS – brown 16lb 2oz and rainbow 30lb 12oz.

FACILITIES – there's a lodge and good meals at an on-site pub. Tea and coffee are free. A tackle shop stocks virtually all you need and the farm shop sells trout if you can't catch any!

→ DIRECTIONS – from Tavistock, head north on the A386 along the edge of Dartmoor towards Okehampton. About a mile past the grounds of Kelly College, you will find the fishery on your left. The car park is opposite.

ACCOMMODATION – there is holiday accommodation on site or phone the Tourist Information Centre in Tavistock on 01822 612938.

SEA TROUT RIVERS OF THE SOUTH WEST

Where do you start to describe the sea trout delights of this part of the world, given that there are at least fifty rivers worthy of mention in Devon, Cornwall and Somerset? Before I go any further, I ought to point out that salmon and brown trout are present in many of these rivers as well. But it's the sea trout that make these rivers so special, especially in this day and age when rivers elsewhere in Britain are frequently experiencing failing runs. Of course, down in the South West there are inevitably problems – many of them brought about, no doubt, by the change in this country's climatic patterns. Whereas we once talked about spring-, summer- and autumn-run fish, it's much more difficult nowadays to draw the distinctions... global warming, call it what you will, has changed the old patterns of behaviour.

Nonetheless, providing these south-west rivers get some rain early in the year, there are still runs of fish, and these are often plentiful. Many of the school sea trout are only one and a half to two and a half pounds, but some of the rivers – for example the Tavy – experience vast numbers of fish in the five- to six-pound region, as well as fish that run into double figures.

Sea trout tend to rest up in deeper pools during the day and then move up river during the hours of darkness, and the moving fish are generally the ones that can be caught. For this reason, most sea trout fishing takes place after dusk, but do make sure you spy out the land in advance. It's no fun stumbling around in the dark wondering where the hell you are!

A longish rod between ten and eleven feet is about right – it gives that little bit more control over hard-fighting fish, and it means you barely have to cast when you want to put out a short line. And short lines are best. Don't be too over-ambitious casting in the dark, especially on a river that's new to you. Keep it short and tight, and move as gently and quietly as you can. Favoured patterns include the Alexandra, the Bloody Butcher, the Teal Blue and Silver, Medicine and Peter Ross. I like using muddlers when fish are moving on the surface. Larger, traditional dry flies can appeal, too, often when there's a full moon and/or thundery weather and the barometer's high.

A couple of last tips: even if the days have been warm, the nights can be cool. Thermal underwear helps to keep the chill away and a flask of tea provides inner warmth. Make sure you take insect repellent – midges can be maddening on still nights. Don't forget a small torch – necessary for tying knots and selecting flies – and it's never a bad idea to paint the rim of your landing net white. This makes it much easier to see in the dark and it's a tip that's saved many an angler a last-ditch, struggling, six-pound sea trout!

But where exactly should you fish? The region's excellent rivers include the Dart, the Fowey, the Lyn, the Plym, the Tamar, the Tavy and the Torridge. That's not to say there aren't others, but has anyone fished the lot?

SEASON – The season for migratory trout does vary to some degree. Most of the rivers open in either March or April but the general closing date is 30 September. Check local restrictions when making enquiries.

TICKETS – Many of the waters are tightly controlled and access can be limited. However, contact South-west Water Leisure Services for detailed advice. Permits for the Tavy, the Walkham and Plym can be obtained from Barkells, 15 Duke Street, Tavistock PL19 0BA. Contact Two Bridges Hotel, just outside Princetown, on 01822 890581 for tickets for the Dart. The Prince Hall Hotel in Princetown, on 01822 890403, also offers tickets for the Dart, as does the Forest Inn, Hexworthy, PL20 6SD, which can be reached on 01364 631211. The Ensly House Hotel at Milton Abbot, Devon PL19 0PQ has permits on the Tamar. For the Taw, try the Rising Sun Hotel at Umberleigh, on 01769 560447, and the Fox and Hounds Hotel at Eggsford, Devon.

⇒ SEA TROUT IN THE DAYTIME ⇐

Sea trout fishing is traditionally carried out at night but increasingly anglers are looking for sport during the daytime. And by using the right tactics, they are finding it! Here's how:

- *Move very, very cautiously. Daytime sea trout are particularly fidgety and prone to alarm.*
- *It's important to target your fish by finding them first and not casting haphazardly. Unnecessary casts will only spook the shoal.*
- *You'll find that even large sea trout are willing to come up to take a fly from the surface. But the flies must be small. Try something on a size 14 or 16. Cast well upstream and give the fish plenty of time to see it.*
- *If you can't get the fish to come up, then don't hesitate to get a fly down to where they're lying. Go for something with a bit of vim and vigour. Try a big Goldhead or even a Montana. What you're looking for is something that makes a bit of a plop and goes down very fast indeed.*
- *Try casting directly into the shoal or immediately in front of a specific fish and watch the fly go down.*
- *You'll either get an immediate take… or it will be a disaster and the entire shoal will take fright. If this is the case, don't carry on scaring the fish. You've got to think of those anglers who are out on the bank after dusk, and they don't want to come across heavily spooked trout.*
- *That's the mystery of sea trout – sometimes they'll take during the day and sometimes they won't. They know their own mind and there's little we can do to change it.*

▭ **ACCOMMODATION** – There is a wide variety of bed and breakfast, self-catering and hotel accommodation in this bustling tourist area. Contact the Dartmoor Tourist Association at the Duchy Building, Tavistock Road, Princetown, Plymouth, Devon PL20 6QF, on 01822 890567. Contact the Tourist Information Centre in Plymouth, on 01752 304849, for more general advice on accommodation in the area.

WATERCRESS FARM FISHERY – DEVON

Watercress Farm boasts three lakes, all very well matured, with one of them going back nearly fifty years. The lakes are all spring-fed, which helps explain their crystal-clear qualities. The water is very rich, with abundant weed growth and a big range of insect life. Depths range from around four feet to fourteen on average, but there are plenty of deeper holes that the fish look to in bright, warm weather. The largest lake, Ash, runs down to thirty feet, whereas the central lake, Oak, has extensive margins only a couple of feet deep or so and running down to fifteen feet. This allows for a great range of insect life. Alder, the most recent lake, has depths to about ten feet.

The lakes are also surrounded by abundant tree growth, so there are plenty of terrestrials blown off into the water – hence the popularity of the Flying Ant and the Black Fly for those liking to fish on the top.

Watercress sees big hatches of buzzers, and many of the locals fish little else. However, damsel nymphs and Montanas all catch a good number. The basic rule at Watercress is to fish tight and inconspicuously, remembering that if you can see the fish, there's a good chance that they can see you.

Watercress does not stand still, and at present one of the lakes is extensively stocked with brown trout, brook trout and tiger trout to provide welcome alternatives to the ubiquitous rainbow. This lake does have a closed season – from October through to March – but the others are open all year. Most stocked fish are around two pounds but a sixteen-and-a-half-pound trout has recently been caught, with innumerable ten-pound plus fish.

☼ **SEASON** – the fishery is open the year round.

✦ **TICKETS** – phone 01626 852168 for prior booking or write to Watercress Farm Fishery, Kerswells Chudleigh, Newton Abbot, Devon. A five-fish limit costs £21, a four-fish limit £17, a three-fish limit £15 and an evening ticket (two-fish limit, from 5pm) £12.

→ **DIRECTIONS** – leave the M5 onto the A38 Exeter to Plymouth road. Leave the A38 onto the B3344 road and the lane that goes past Watercress Farm is between the Highwayman's Haunt and the entrance to the caravan park. It's well signposted.

▭ **ACCOMMODATION** – there is a caravan park next to the fishery – Holman's Wood – but the major centres of Torquay and Paignton are close at hand. Phone the Tourist Information Centre in Torquay on 0906 680 1268 for further details of various kinds of accommodation.

THE RESERVOIRS OF SOMERSET

True, Blagdon, Chew and Wimbleball are all geographically closely sited, but they each have their own unique character. What they do share is fascinating fishing for well-conditioned fish in dramatic countryside. They're all very good-sized waters – Chew comes in at twelve hundred acres, Blagdon almost four hundred and fifty acres and Wimbleball nearly four hundred... so there's plenty of bank and boat fishing to explore. There is prolific fly life on all three reservoirs and that, combined with very good stocking levels, gives you every chance of a good day's fishing.

Obviously, all the usual techniques work on these reservoirs, but what is not so often tried is dry fly fishing, a real winner in the summer months and into the early autumn. Indeed, from the end of April, providing the weather is warm, dry flies begin to work with a vengeance. Look out for wind and scum lanes, because both of these hold food and the trout will never be far away nor, even more importantly, far from the surface in these areas.

Remember when you're fishing dry flies to cast them accurately, speedily and with a good presentation. Look very carefully at the route that the rising trout is taking and try to present your fly a couple of feet or so in front of where you guess its nose is likely to be. Never cast directly at the ring of the last rise, because the fish will have moved on and you'll be casting behind it.

An overcast, warm day with a light wind is perfect. If it's overcast but windy, simply step up the size of the flies on your leader. In flat calms, don't cast too often because all you'll do is disturb the water. Wait till you see a fish move and then cast in one gentle, unhurried movement. Other tips? When a trout takes your fly, delay for a split second and then strike, even though you won't feel a pull on the hand. Always degrease your leader with a mixture of Fuller's Earth and washing-up liquid so that it sinks beneath the surface.

Remember, too, to grease your dry fly with a floatant – spray it or rub it onto your finger first and then apply to the fly. And as for choosing the right fly, well, there are endless possible patterns, so it really pays to take the advice of the bailiffs on the water. If I had to choose a favourite for much of the year, it would have to be the simple Black Gnat. If you're getting refusals, it could be that your fly is too big – going down a couple of sizes might work.

So, a few tips for exciting fishing on three of the most lovely reservoirs that you'll come across in the South West – or anywhere else, come to that.

SEASON – in essence, you're allowed to fish from April through to November, but there are various restrictions on taking brown trout. On Chew, for example, boat fishing ends on 29 October and bank fishing on 26 November. Fishing is until sunset or one hour afterwards on all three reservoirs.

TICKETS – Chew and Blagdon are controlled by Bristol Water PLC, Recreations

Department, Woodford Lodge, Chew Stoke, Bristol BS18 8XH. You can contact them on 01275 332339. Permits are available in advance, from the lodges or from ticket machines. For fishing on Wimbleball Lake, phone Lance Nicholson, High Street, Dulverton, Somerset, on 01398 323409. There is a whole range of ticket prices. For example, on Chew a boat day permit is £55 for two rods. This includes boat hire, fishing tickets and a total of 16 fish.

¶† FACILITIES – All three reservoirs have lodges, well-maintained boats, weighing stations and so on. But you should also be aware that on each there are areas out of bounds to fishermen. These are all important nature reserves and it's essential, for the reputation of angling, to observe the 'no go' areas.

→ DIRECTIONS – Both Chew and Blagdon are situated to the south west of Bristol, just off the A368, midway between Bath and Weston-Super-Mare. They are well signposted, and there are plenty of car parks. Wimbleball is situated to the east of Dulverton and the south of Brompton Regis. It is best reached from the B3190, which runs from Brampton northwards towards Watchet.

⊢⊣ ACCOMMODATION – The local Tourist Information Centres will give details on various kinds of accommodation available in the area. Phone the Bristol office on 0117 926 0767 or Tiverton on 01884 255827.

❧ HIGHLY RECOMMENDED FISHERIES ❧

- *Bellbrook Valley Trout Fishery, Nr. Exbridge, Devon. 01398 351292. Beautiful string of peaceful, scenic lakes, liberally stocked with doubles.*
- *Blakewell Fishery. Can be contacted on 01271 344533. Good morning and evening buzzer water.*
- *Tavistock Trout Fishery, Devon. Phone 01822 615441. A really big fish lake. Fish to twenty pounds plus.*
- *Rose Park Trout Fishery, Cornwall. Phone 01566 86278 for details. Some nice fish. Pleasant surroundings and a warm welcome.*
- *Siblyback Reservoir. Details on 01579 342366. An attractive reservoir, fished very well from a boat.*
- *Quantock Fishery, Somerset. Phone 01823 451367. An excellent mix of varieties – rainbows, browns and tigers.*
- *Hawkridge Reservoir, Somerset. Details can be obtained on 01278 671840. A beautiful water.*
- *Clatworthy Reservoir. An established water and a really good challenge.*

Fly-Fishing Sites
in the South

1. Avon Springs Fishery
2. The Rivers Test and Itchen
3. Moorhen Trout Fishery
4. Avington Trout Fisheries
5. Rooksbury Mill
6. Felix Farm

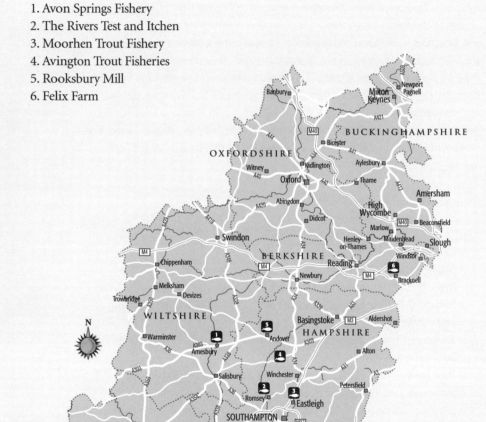

'To the chalk-stream fisherman, June is the best month of all, for who would not, if he could, choose a windless day in June? It is a month of the meadow flowers, and though the different shades of green are less marked and emerging into their summer sameness, the yellow iris makes the banks a garden, the wild rose stars the hedges and the guelder rose hangs its green-coloured lamps over the carriers.'

J . W. HILLS, *A SUMMER ON THE TEST*, 1924

The southern counties and trout fishing are synonymous, and rivers such as the Test and Itchen have a fundamental place at the heart of the sport for game fishermen. These were, in many ways, the cradle of fly fishing. It was here that modern dry fly fishing and nymphing were brought to fruition.

There's something about the water quality – not just the rivers – of these southern counties. Perhaps it's because the water often runs from chalk and is crystal clear and immensely fertile. As a result, the fish grow big and are habitually cunning, and anglers are able to see just where they've been going wrong.

When you think of southern England, it's the rivers that spring to mind, but this is not to say that there aren't some fabulous still-water fisheries. If anything, these lakes are even clearer than the rivers, and the fish can be every bit as difficult to deceive. At certain fisheries – such as Avington – the angler has the best of both worlds and can move from still water to river. The southern counties are places where every valley has a twinkling stream and every fly fisherman goes home fulfilled.

The South offers an intriguing mix of enormous, artificially-bred rainbow trout and immaculate wild fish. For example, you will find rivers where wild browns still spawn naturally. A short distance away, there may be a lake that has just been stocked with rainbows of double figures. Both extremes of the sport offer a great deal. This is a broad church indeed.

AVON SPRINGS FISHERY – WILTSHIRE

Avon Springs really shows what commercial fisheries can aspire to. There are two lakes here, one of five acres and one of three acres, in conjunction with four miles of the upper Avon. And what fishing we're talking about. The water is crystal clear, very prolific, with good weed growth. And the fish are sensational. As I write, the average – yes, the average – size of the rainbows is just over six pounds. The browns are not far behind, and there are double-figure fish of both species to be caught. In fact, limit bags of thirty pounds plus are going out every week.

In part, this is down to the stocking policy, but the fish do extraordinarily well in the water and many of them over-winter to become perfect specimens. Naturally enough, damsels work very well, especially when stalking, but most years there is an excellent mayfly hatch, along with prolific hawthorn, so there's the opportunity for really thrilling surface fishing too.

The river also deserves mention. There's a very good head of wild-bred brown trout. And the grayling really get your mouth watering. The average size is something between a pound and a pound and a half, but plenty of fish of two to two and a half pounds plus are taken.

☀ SEASON – open all year.

🐟 TICKETS – contact Avon Springs Fishery, Recreation Road, Durrington, Salisbury, Wiltshire, SP4 8EZ. A full-day ticket is £38 (four-fish limit), a half-day ticket is £30 (three-fish limit) and an evening ticket is £20 (two-fish limit). There is no catch and release. Grayling fishing is allowed on the river throughout the winter on a £40-a-day sporting ticket. Everything must go back. Details on 01980 653557.

→ DIRECTIONS – following the A303 from Exeter to London, turn left at Amesbury along the A345. You will come to a roundabout with the Stonehenge pub opposite. Turn right and follow this road until you get to Rangers Garage on the left. Turn left and Recreation Road is the third on the right with the lakes well signposted.

🛏 ACCOMMODATION – details of various kinds of accommodation in the Salisbury area can be obtained from the Tourist Information Centre on 01722 334956.

THE SOUTHERN RIVERS

Okay, just conceivably, these are not what they once were and, yes, abstraction and long-term, insidious pollution have had some undesirable effects on these rivers, but the chalk rivers of the south are still a fly-fisher's paradise: the Upper Avon and its tributaries; the Wylye and the Nadder; the Itchen; the Test; the Kennet. These are just a few. Crystal clear, running over chalk, gravel and sand. Prolific weed growth. Abundant fly life. Large, perfectly-formed, cunning fish. Trout fishing at its best.

The Itchen is perhaps the jewel of all the Wessex chalk streams. Stunningly clear and rich in insect life, it breeds trout of majestic size and with awesome discriminatory powers.

Trotting the stream for grayling in the autumn time is one of the game fisher's most unexpected pleasures. All right, it's not fly-fishing as such, but it's still an art to be mastered.

The twinkling rivers of Exmoor, such as the Barle, may well be small but they hold exciting fish stocks. In late summer, runs of grilse flock the river and year round there are delightful wild brown trout.

Action on the Test. The River Test is synonymous with English fly-fishing and, although it has been preserved for centuries, there are still day ticket opportunities available.

The Derbyshire Dove, on a crisp morning when the frost crackles underfoot and the grayling sip in tiny wet flies, offers excellent sport to warm the cockles of your heart.

The magnificent estate of Chatsworth provides stunning summer trout fishing and magnificent grayling throughout the winter. Day tickets are available for the lucky residents of the Cavendish Hotel.

The fisheries here have a history. These are the streams of Halford, Skues, Sawyer and Dermot Wilson. These are the places where dry fly and nymphing were both brought to their present state of art. These are the rivers where entomology really first made its big impact on fly fishing. It's on these rivers that some of the very best books on fly fishing ever have been written – witness *Where the Bright Waters Meet* and *A Summer on the Test*.

Highlights... the mayfly season, those two weeks around the end of May and the beginning of June when the valleys are a cascade of golden-glowing insects. Spirals and spirals of mayflies turning the air into a shifting fog. Mayflies falling so thick that cars have to be driven with windscreen wipers turned on high. Rivers coated in the dead insects and trout fat as pigs from the fortnight's feast.

Highlights... men like Ron Holloway, river keepers with a lifetime's experience. Men of passion, men with a commitment to keeping these rivers as pristine as God intended them. Listen to Ron as he tells you how he tends his river and you'll feel there isn't a single grain of gravel he hasn't examined, polished and returned to best effect. Brown trout are his passion, wild brown trout, fish that can still breed freely in a river where they know their fry and fingerlings will be protected.

Highlights... an evening rise, countryside so beautiful you think your heart will break. Watching great browns hanging suspended in water as clear as air. Watching your upstream nymph disappear in a flash of white mouth. And, even if you can't get on some of the most hallowed stretches in the summer, there's a chance for you when it comes to winter grayling.

Grayling aren't always welcome visitors, not even now in the 21st century, but mostly they're tolerated. And what grayling they are... two pounders are common, three pounders are there to be caught, and in huge numbers.

I remember very well a late January afternoon on the Lambourne when I took my first two-pound grayling on the fly from a little weir pool on a carrier. Twenty minutes later I'd taken three. Two pounds two ounces, two pounds five ounces and two pounds seven ounces. Then there was the walk home, through the frost-crackling wood where the pheasants called, and up the high street of the sleepy little rural village to my homely bed and breakfast.

The joys of the southern rivers are infinite. Of course, access is as jealously guarded as the keys to the crown jewels, but it can be done. For a price – and not always an exorbitant one – you can find yourself a day in paradise.

☀ **Seasons** – I'm not really going to comment on the seasons for the chalk streams simply because so many fisheries have their own rules and regulations. This is especially true when it comes to the grayling.

🐟 **Tickets** – Roxton Bailey Robinson, High Street, Hungerford, RG17 0NF is a good starting point for beats on the Test. Phone 01488 683222 for details. It's also worth contacting the Estate Office, Broadlands, Romsey, SO51 9ZE. Call them on 01794 518885. Contact also Roy Gumbrell on 01264 810833 at The Greyhound Inn, Stockbridge, Hampshire. Call Fishing Breaks Ltd., who also control fishing on the Test, Avon, Itchen and Dever, on 020 7359 8818. Alternatively, write to them at 16 Bickerton Road, London N19 5JR. Perhaps the most important address of all is that excellent tackle shop, The Rod Box, London Road, King's Worthy, Winchester. This excellent shop – where everyone seems to be a mine of information and enthusiastic help – controls several beats on the Itchen, Test, Bourne and Whitewater. Phone 01962 883600 for more details.

🛏 **Accommodation** – the Tourist Information Centres in Winchester, on 01962 840500, and Southampton, on 023 8022 1106, will be able to give details of accommodation available in the area, from bed and breakfasts to luxury hotels.

❧ Building up Knowledge ❧

- You can't really do much better than getting out on the bankside with an acknowledged expert. It doesn't matter how much you read, you can't beat the hands-on approach. There are a good number of instructors around the country, including Gavin Hodgson, 0118 930 3860 at Sportfish, Reading and Bob James, who gives occasional courses at the Caer Beris Manor Hotel. Phone 01982 552601 for details.
- Game anglers are also fortunate in the quality of magazines on their newsagents' shelves. **Trout Fisherman** is long established and really does point any trout angler in the right direction. **Trout and Salmon** has been highly respected for many years now and offers a very good overview of the game fishing scene. **Total Fly Fishing** looks like being an important newcomer.
- Try to get to the fairs. The Chatsworth Fly Fishing Fair and the CLA Game Fair offer excellent opportunities to meet skilled fly fishermen and to benefit from casting clinics. The Fisherman's Village at the Game Fair is really worth a visit.

Moorhen Trout Fishery – Hampshire

Despite my liking for catch and release, it can be a problem for fishery owners, especially when the fish are very large. This proved the case at Moorhen. Going back just a handful of years, it was a renowned big fish water, but the problem was that sometimes the big fish just weren't handled well – understandable, I suppose, in the excitement of the moment – and they were returned only to sink and die. Not good for the fish and also not good for the fishery – and very bad for finances. As a result, Moorhen has reverted to a neater and more manageable type of fishery.

What makes Moorhen so appealing is its stunning appearance. The water isn't large – about two and a half acres – but its setting is really superb. Go there on a pleasant, bright day and I swear you won't be disappointed. The welcome, too, is very warm, and the lodge is well laid out and functional.

Today, Moorhen operates with stocked fish – in beautiful condition – of between one and a half and two pounds, with a number of fish in the five- to six-pound bracket to be caught. Floating lines are generally all that is needed, and buzzers, dries and other imitative patterns do the business. Barbless hooks are, by the way, obligatory – a wise rule indeed.

⌂ **Season** – open all year.

🦐 **Tickets** – the Fishery Manager, Moorhen Lake, Warnford, Nr. Southampton, Hampshire. Phone 01730 829460 for details. Day tickets are £40 for four fish, £25 for three fish and £15 for two fish. Catch and release.

→ **Directions** – leave the M27 at junction 10 and take the A32 towards Alton. The entrance to the fishery lies right on the road on the left hand side just out of the village of Warnford.

🛏 **Accommodation** – the Tourist Information Centre in Southampton, on 023 8022 1106, can supply information on various kinds of accommodation in the area.

Avington Trout Fisheries – Hampshire

Avington was opened for trout fishing way back in 1967, so it is, in many ways, one of the forerunners of all commercial trout fisheries. It's certainly among the most famous for its extraordinary stocking policies... huge and perfectly-formed rainbows are very much the order of the day here. Avington is made up of two lakes – one of two acres and one of four acres – and they are both fed by the River Itchen that runs nearby. Indeed, the fishery includes half a mile of Itchen carrier, although this is seldom stocked. Avington is a beautiful, secluded place ringed by trees, the margins dotted with yellow flag. You really are in a glorious piece of Hampshire countryside at Avington.

The rainbows are reared from fingerlings on site and this, combined with brilliant water quality, makes for fascinating and exceptionally fine rainbows. Mind you, even though stocking is generous and sight fishing is possible, the fishing is far from easy. A four-fish limit really has to be striven for.

A gold-headed damsel nymph is always a good starter – as it is anywhere. Fish here also come up for buzzers and small white and black lures. If you're going to fish Avington like an expert, however, think about heavily leaded bugs and nymphs that you can drop in front of a fish knowing they will get to the required depth quickly. That's one of the secrets of stalking – you've got to put your fly at the right level. Of course, there's a lot more to it, and in the first place you've got to see your fish! Try to get as high as possible to see down into the water – perhaps step up on a bench, making full use of trees behind you to blot out your silhouette. Wear Polaroids and a broad-peaked cap to help cut down the light. Move carefully, scanning the water as you go.

Look around weed beds, particularly, and under the trees at Avington. You'll find a lot of fish in the margins, too. Once you've spotted one that you'd like to target, get down low and watch it carefully as you build up a picture of its patrol route. Once you have this, you can drop the fly just ahead of its imminent arrival. That way you won't spook the fish so much.

Look for fish close in if you're new to this, because accurate casting is everything. If you're going to cast twenty yards or more, you'll need quite a bit of skill and experience to get the fly right on the rainbow's nose.

Obviously, you want to go as light as you possibly can, but remember that some of these Avington fish reach twenty pounds, and if there's a lot of weed about.... Try, wherever possible, once a fish is hooked, to play it off the reel. It's common to play trout by the hand but this leaves loops of line all over the place, which it's all too easy to step on just as a big fish makes another surge for freedom. Keep using side strain, as this knocks the fish off balance and tires it out more quickly. You've also got to choose the right day: bright light and gentle winds are ideal for seeing down into the crystal depths. But, most importantly, remember your manners. Don't encroach on anybody else's fishing space – not even if you're following a big fish that you think has your name on it. Remember that everybody's paid for their ticket. It's easy to think that stalking is somehow a superior sport reserved for the gods... it isn't. It's just a very satisfying way of reaching your limit bag.

 SEASON – open all year, seven days a week. The fishery is open from 8.00am until dusk.

 TICKETS – contact the Fishery Trout Manager on 019627 79312 at Avington Trout Fishery, Avington, Winchester, Hants SO21 1BZ. A day ticket is £60 for four fish. An afternoon ticket £35 for two fish. There is no catch and release.

→ DIRECTIONS – leave the M3 at junction 9 and turn onto the A31 towards Farnham. The road down to Avington and Itchen Abbas is on the left.

 ACCOMMODATION – contact the Tourist Information Centre in Winchester on 01962 840500 for details of accommodation available in the area.

ROOKSBURY MILL – HAMPSHIRE

Rooksbury has built up a great reputation over the years as a fabulous, big-fish water in tremendous surroundings. It is now owned by Test Valley Borough Council and has a self-sustaining population of fish. There are two lakes within magnificent surroundings; a six-acre fishing lake with maximum depths going down to twelve or fourteen feet and a three-acre lake, now left as a conservation lake. The lakes are crystal clear and spring-fed: the effect of the springs is to push the fish up towards the surface layers; even in winter you'll find them most active in the top three feet of water.

For this reason, all you'll ever need at Rooksbury is a floating line and long leader. A couple of years back, a survey was taken of all the catch returns, and the top three flies proved to be damsel imitations, Green Montanas and gold-ribbed Hare's Ears, with Sawyer nymphs coming in fourth. A slow, careful retrieve is probably the best way to lure these fine fish, which average between four and five pounds in weight.

The stretch of the River Anton in Rooksbury Mill is out of bounds for conservation reasons. The fish community at Rooksbury Mill is comprised of roach, tench, perch, carp, pikes, eels and grayling.

 SEASON – the fishery is open all year round.

 TICKETS – available from Chalis Tackle in Andover, Hampshire at £6 per day for one rod and £8 per day for two rods.

→ DIRECTIONS – come off the A303 Exeter to London Road and take the A3057 towards Andover. Turn left down Wellesly Road, drive to the end and take a left along Barlows Lane. Rooksbury Mill car park is signposted on the right.

 ACCOMMODATION – the Tourist Information Centre in Andover, on 01264 324320, will be able to supply a list of available accommodation. Alternatively, contact the Winchester Tourist Information Centre on 01962 840500 or the Salisbury Tourist Information Centre on 01722 334956.

FELIX FARM – BERKSHIRE

Felix Farm was dug back in the seventies to provide gravel for the nearby M4. It's now a very mature ten-acre lake with a firm following of regular visitors. A lot of the water is surprisingly shallow for an old gravel pit, but there are good areas that dip to twenty feet or so. These are fishable from one of the boats, which must be moored up at well-positioned buoys.

Felix Farm is spring-fed and has a constant water supply, and it is clear enough for heart-stopping stalking techniques to be used. The trout are stocked on a daily basis – probably averaging around the two-pound mark – but bigger fish go in every week. It's a prolific water: there are buzzer hatches throughout the year, even in winter, along with hawthorns and mayfly, which generally appear in June. Naturally enough, this means that surface fishing with buzzers and dries is one of the most effective methods. Try the Grey Wolf tied on a size fourteen. Sedge patterns also work well, but don't go too light on your leader strength; there are some hefty trout about. This is a pretty, well-thought-out fishery with a very nice stamp of fish indeed. Try it!

SEASON – open all year including bank holidays, 8.00am to dusk.

TICKETS – contact Martin Suddards on 01189 345527 or write to him at Felix Farm Trout Fishery, Howe Lane, Binfield, Bracknell Berkshire, RG 42 5QL. Day tickets are £25 (five-fish limit), half-day tickets are £22 (three-fish limit), short-day or evening tickets are £18 (four hours, two-fish limit) and novice/oap tickets are £15 (two-fish limit). It is advisable to phone and make a booking. The fishery only takes about 18 people.

DIRECTIONS – leave the M4 at junction 8/9 and take the A308 for Windsor, then the Bracknell and Ascot road through Hollyport and Touchen End. Take the right hand fork and you will pass the Win Again pub on the Twyford road. After a mile, turn left for Binfield. The entrance to the fishery is opposite the Jolly Farmer pub.

ACCOMMODATION – bed and breakfast is available at Felix Farm. Contact the Tourist Information Centre at Bracknell on 01344 868196 for other accommodation in the area.

❧ HIGHLY RECOMMENDED FISHERIES ❧

- *Hazelcopse, Nr. Ridgwick, Surrey. Call 01403 822878 for details. Two attractive lakes offering huge browns, rainbows and still water salmon.*
- *Chiphall Lake, Fareham, Hants. Phone 01329 833295. Crystal stalking water in the Meon valley. Big rainbows.*
- *Leominstead Trout Fishery, Lyndhurst, Hants. Phone 02380 282610 for information. Very pretty, well-stocked water.*
- *Frensham Trout Fishery, Surrey. Call 01252 794321. Great in autumn.*
- *Albury. Call 01483 202323 for details. Super water. Tremendous fishing. Highly recommended.*
- *Coltsford Mill, Surrey. Phone 01883 715666 for details. Excellent facilities and some very big fish.*
- *John O'Gaunts. Phone 01794 388130. A tremendous water with high average weight. Highly recommended.*
- *Dever Springs, Hampshire. Details can be obtained on 01264 720592. The original huge-fish water. An amazing experience. Visit at least once!*
- *Meon Springs, Hampshire. Contact on 01730 823249. Great visibility, great stock of fish and great welcome.*

FLY-FISHING SITES IN THE SOUTH EAST

1. Chalk Springs Trout Fishery
2. Bewl Water
3. Halliford Mere
4. Syon Park Fishery
5. Walthamstow Reservoir
6. Rib Valley Fishery
7. Norton Fishery
8. Brickhouse Farm
9. Hanningfield Reservoir
10. Clavering Lake

*And, next, I shall tell you, that it is observed…
that there is no better Salmon than in England; and
that though some of our northern counties have as fat,
and as large, as the river Thames, yet none are
of so excellent a taste…
There are also, in divers rivers, especially that relate to,
or be near to the sea, as Winchester, or the Thames about
Windsor, a little Trout called a Samlet, or Skegger Trout,
in both which places I have caught twenty or forty at a
standing, that will bite as fast and as freely as Minnows:
these be by some taken to be young Salmons.*

IZAAK WALTON, *THE COMPLEAT ANGLER*, 1653

A ny reader of Izaak Walton's *Compleat Angler* will know that back in the seventeenth century a fisherman could find his heart's content within strolling distance of Charing Cross. This was a time when apprentices revolted against the monotony of their daily fare of salmon, and when any number of small streams ran in and around the capital, all holding trout.

Things were to change dramatically, however, and by the 1850s, Walton wouldn't have known the rivers and streams that he once so happily fished. The rapid population increase – and more importantly, its sewage – just about destroyed the Londoner's Thames, and for the next century, the situation got little better. Now, however, for a man in London with a fly rod the prospects are nowhere near as bleak. A twenty-first-century Walton might well not be able to find as many wild fish – or indeed any – but there will still be places to delight his heart.

The growth of commercial trout fisheries has been a phenomenon, and there can have been few places in Britain to have profited as much as London. Now, you can hop on the tube and fish a delightful day at Syon Park or take a bus out to Walthamstow and enjoy yourself on the trout-filled reservoirs.

CHALK SPRINGS TROUT FISHERY – SUSSEX

I've only actually fished Chalk Springs once, but it was a day of pleasure that I could never forget. Okay, the weather was warm and sunny, which always helps, but there's far more that sticks in the mind. In short, Chalk Springs offers something for everybody. The four lakes there cater for the inexperienced fisherman as well as the man who wants a real challenge. I had my kicks stalking a fish of around four pounds in gin-clear water over luxuriant weed growth with four or five different sort of flies... and I failed.

No matter, there were all manner of other very attractive looking fish for me to go for. Finally, I succeeded with a rainbow of about two and three quarter pounds that fought magnificently and looked even better. And some trout that I watched in the adjoining lake looked at the twelve-pound mark.

Obviously fish will come to the lure at Chalk Springs, but I really think that small, imitative patterns are all that's really needed. You won't need a sinking line – you won't find water anywhere deeper than ten to fifteen feet – though a long leader is sometimes a good idea to get down deep to fish that are sulking in the heat of the day. The fishery is very friendly and you're made to feel a welcome guest. A glorious place to while away a splendid day.

SEASON – Chalk Springs is open all year including Bank Holidays, but do book in advance. The lakes are quite small and a limited number of tickets are issued. The fishery opens at 8.30am and closes at dusk.

TICKETS – apply to Darren Smith at Chalk Springs Trout Fishery, Park Bottom, Arundel, West Sussex, BN18 0AA or phone 01903 883742. Adult day-ticket prices start from around £38 but there are cheaper alternatives. There are concessions for juniors and senior citizens.

RECORDS – brown trout 19lb, rainbow trout 20lb 9oz, tiger trout 14lb 2oz and blue trout 17lb 6oz.

DIRECTIONS – if you take the A27 from Worthing and Brighton to Arundel and then bypass the town, you will cross the river and come to a roundabout. Continue along the A27, signposted Chichester. After a short distance, you will see the lodge on the right-hand side and signs to Chalk Springs. If you reach the hospital, you have gone too far.

ACCOMMODATION – lists of accommodation available in Arundel and the surrounding area can be obtained from the Tourist Information Centre in Arundel on 01903 882268.

BEWL WATER – KENT

Bewl Water is the largest inland water in the south-east of England. Its seventeen miles of bankside can be intimidating for visiting anglers, at least until you get to know it. This is rather a shame because, in actual fact, Bewl is both outstandingly beautiful and very generously stocked. Indeed, Bewl is much more intimate than its size might suggest, and this is down to the many bays that divide the water up and give it an exceptional character. What's more, at Bewl you can always find somewhere to get out of the wind and the chances are that you'll probably have a little cove pretty much to yourself. And what lovely names the bays have... Goose Creek, Tinkers' Marsh, The Nose... there's enough magic and mystery there for anyone!

Bewl is a working reservoir, so it can be subject to a significant draw down during hot summer months when water is in short supply, and it's then that weed growth can be a problem, especially for bank anglers. If you're thinking of visiting Bewl during July or August, a boat may be a good idea. Mind you, if you're happier on the bank, don't worry too much – the trout will come into the fertile shallows and they'll feed there throughout the day, especially if there hasn't been much disturbance. If you can get out early and stay until last knockings, then you'll find the best of the bankside sport.

All forms of fly fishing can score at Bewl. Lure stripping – especially with a muddler minnow on calm days – will have an impact. Nymphing, though, is favourite. Also, try dry flies, especially in high summer towards dusk when buzzers also come into their own. It pays to keep on the move. If you move around a bit you're much more likely to come across a group of fish that probably haven't been attempted for a day or two.

Local knowledge is always essential and here at Bewl the staff really do know their stuff. Indeed, if it's a little instruction that you think your fly fishing could do with, Bewl is the perfect place. It has deservedly gained an enviable reputation for its excellent one-day courses. There is a beginners' course, a junior fly-fishing course and a very useful problem-solving course, designed for those with some experience, who wish to improve their casting.

Bewl is also the perfect place for a family day out. For example, the *Frances Mary* boat offers a cruise around the reservoir for a very modest charge. There are walks, picnic areas, woodland playgrounds and so on. And it's all in a designated 'Area of Outstanding Natural Beauty', so you're likely to see a wealth of birdlife and even a fox or wild deer. Given that Bewl stocks annually with over fifty thousand trout and produces double-figure browns and rainbows, you couldn't wish for a better fly fishing venue.

SEASON – Bewl opens on 21 March and closes around 17 November. Bank fishing takes place from sunrise to one hour after sunset. Boat fishing begins at 9.00am and finishes at 10.00pm or one hour after sunset, whichever is earlier.

TICKETS – these are available from the Fishing Lodge, Bewl Water, Lamberhurst, Kent TN3 8JH. There is a scale of charges but a basic day ticket that gives an eight-fish limit bag costs £18.20. Motor boats are available for around £23.20 a day and rowing boats for around £13.50. Phone 01892 890352 for the entire list of charges. Though the fishing fleet runs to about fifty boats in its entirety, prior booking is still recommended.

→ **DIRECTIONS** – access to the fishing lodge is via the A21 London to Hastings road and Bewl Bridge Lane. Then follow the signs on site.

⊨ **ACCOMMODATION** – the Tourist Information Office in Tunbridge Wells will provide information on accommodation in the area. Phone 01892 515675 for details.

HALLIFORD MERE – MIDDLESEX

Halliford is a really useful water for Londoners and for visitors to the capital. The main reason for this is its very enlightened policy towards fishing. Halliford is now virtually totally catch and release, although you can take fish from one lake at a cost of £2 per head. But, for the rest, the fish go back. According to Bill Berwick, the owner, it's a popular system: 'Okay, we've lost a few die-hards by changing our policy, but we've picked up far more people than we've lost. Most people, it seems, are fed up with killing things and just seeing them go to waste in deep freezers. It's all right if you definitely want a fish to eat – and we cater for that – but it's a lot more rewarding generally to see a fish swim away free'. I suppose the worry for most fishery owners is how effectively catch and release operates in the summer when water temperatures can climb over eighteen degrees. Bill counters this by pointing out that the fish at this time of the year are much, much more difficult to catch anyway and, I suppose, Halliford Mere, being spring-fed, keeps temperatures to a reasonable level.

But to the fishing… the spring water of Halliford Mere is a major factor in the fabulous fishing. There are about fourteen acres available at Halliford, an original large lake split up into four smaller ones. They're all crystal clear and abound with natural insect life. Damsels, buzzers, shrimps, beetles, corixa… you name it and Halliford Mere will hold it. Twenty feet or so is the extreme in one of the lakes, while the other three rarely dip much below ten or twelve feet. This means that virtually all the regulars use floating lines with longish leaders and that's all you're likely to need, especially as the vast majority of Halliford fish come from the surface.

Yes, it's pretty well all imitative stuff at Halliford. Buzzers, naturally, score highly but there's great dry fly fishing, especially with a variety of sedges. Things change to some degree when the water cools down – from about the middle of October through to March. It's then that lure fishing comes into its own, especially as the trout are increasingly feeding on the coarse fish fry. However, damsel nymphs continue to work, especially fished deeper down.

Winter or summer, it's possible to sight-fish for individual trout. They range between two and eighteen pounds so there are some very interesting ones to target… not that they'll be easy. Most of the fish have been caught at least once or twice in the past and trout certainly learn from their mistakes.

⛅ **Season** – open all year apart from Christmas Day.

🐟 **Tickets** – contact Bill Berwick at Halliford Mere Fishery, Chertsey Road, Shepperton, Middlesex on 01932 253553. Catch and release tickets are available at a blanket price of £20, and these allow you to fish from 8.00am right through to dusk. There is one lake where fish can be taken for £5 per head.

➜ **Directions** – heading south on the M25 towards Gatwick, take junction 11 signposted for Chertsey. Follow the signs for Shepperton and cross over the Thames towards the town. Cross the mini-roundabout and half a mile further on, turn right to Church Square. The entrance will be found shortly afterwards, on the left.

🛏 **Accommodation** – the Tourist Information Centre in Kingston-upon-Thames on 020 8547 5592 will be able to advise on accommodation in the area.

Syon Park Fishery – Middlesex

I've only fished Syon Park once and it was a revelation. I'd actually been to interview the retired ex-butler there – a charming man who showed me round the beautiful house and grounds. The interview went so well that I found myself with a few spare hours, and as I'd got fly tackle in the boot and there was a sparkling lake seconds from the car park, I didn't need much persuading! The whole estate of Syon is a surprise: you don't expect to find such serenity and beauty so close to the M25 and Heathrow.

This very long, thin lake was dug to Capability Brown's plans some two hundred years ago. Like many other estate lakes, it was allowed to silt and decay until a few years back, when the diggers were brought in. Now, it's a sparkling fishery and its shape almost gives you the impression that you're fishing a river. In fact, it is stream-fed: the Duke of Northumberland's River runs in at the far end and out near the car park. This has the benefit of keeping the water cool in the summer and warming it in the winter. Perhaps this is the reason that fish seem to move whatever the weather or season.

Wading is banned here, to help the banksides grow up as wild and natural as possible. This has the added bonus of pulling the fish in close, and you'll often see big, big fish cruising a rod length out. In fact, it's the ideal place to do a bit of stalking. I found it paid to take my time, study the water and not rush in. The locals also reckon that you can get away fishing quite light, and if you use leaders of six pounds or over, you're actually cutting your chances. Of course, if you are going down to four pounds or so, it does mean that you need a light enough rod to cope – especially when you think that the fish are big. The trout, all rainbows, are stocked at two pounds, but there are plenty of doubles and I saw a couple that I'd put at fourteen or fifteen.

All the usual flies work well – damsels, buzzers, daddies, muddler minnows – and if you haven't got what you need in your own fly box, you'll find plenty on offer in the bailiff's own collection. And don't be worried about asking for advice – it will be very freely given. A floating line is probably all you're going to need since Syon has no real depth. There is one area that goes down to about twelve feet, but most of it is around five or six.

All in all, a very attractive, characterful fishery, in lovely surroundings and just a stone's throw from the capital.

 SEASON – open all year apart from 25 and 26 December. The fishery opens at 8.00am and closes at dusk.

 TICKETS – contact Syon Park Fishery, Syon Park, Brentford, Middlesex, TW8 8JF on 020 8568 6354. Andrew Allen is the more than helpful manager. There's a whole range of ticket prices but they begin at £27 for the full day.

 DIRECTIONS – take the A315 west from the Chiswick roundabout on the North Circular at the start of the M4. You will see the sign at the pedestrian entrance for Syon Park – it gives directions for the car entrance lower down. Turn left at the traffic lights on Twickenham Road and drive into the car park. The fishery is near to the well-signposted Butterfly House. Or you can visit by tube – the nearest station is Gunnersbury Park on the District Line.

 ACCOMMODATION – the Tourist Information Centre in Twickenham on 020 8891 7272 will supply details of accommodation in this area.

WALTHAMSTOW AND HANNINGFIELD RESERVOIRS – LONDON AND ESSEX

It would be wrong not to mention these very important reservoirs for the game angler in the South East. They are both very significant in their own ways. Walthamstow Reservoirs 4 and 5, just a few miles from the centre of London, are both available on day ticket and offer huge opportunities for the visitor and local alike. Of course, you're not going to revel in the countryside or feel a million miles from civilisation at Walthamstow. No, these are concrete bowls in the heart of our capital city, but they are full of fish. Lure fishing is generally the most practised of the arts, but the fish will come up to buzzers and dry flies, too, at certain times of the year.

Hanningfield at Chelmsford in Essex is close to the capital, but its six hundred acres of water are much more attractive than Walthamstow's and, vitally, have set a whole new stamp for rainbow trout fishing. Hanningfield's rainbows are simply stunning, crème-de-la-crème rainbows that every other fishery strives to emulate. Fishing at Hanningfield is all about big rainbows. You rarely get one beneath two pounds and they're caught all the way up to twenty pounds and more – the fishery record stands at twenty-four pounds and one ounce. The brown trout are in stupendous condition, too – especially when they edge towards that double-figure mark.

🐟 SEASON – Walthamstow closes between March and June. Hanningfield closes on 31 October and reopens on the last weekend in March.

🎣 TICKETS – for Walthamstow, phone Thames Water on 020 8808 1527. For Hanningfield, contact Hanningfield Trout Fishery, Gifford's Lane, South Hanningfield, Chelmsford, Essex, CM3 8HX, or phone 01245 212034. Day tickets at Hanningfield cost £18.50 with an eight-fish limit, and afternoon tickets cost £15.50 with a four-fish limit. At Walthamstow, a six-fish limit is £20 and a four-fish limit £17.

→ DIRECTIONS – Walthamstow reservoirs can be found just off the A10 going north. Turn right onto the A503 and the reservoirs are alongside the road. Hanningfield lies to the west of the A130. Travelling north towards Chelmsford, look for signposts to South Hanningfield on the left-hand side. The reservoir is well signposted. As it lies only a few miles from Brentwood and the M25, it is still well within range of the tourist visiting London.

🛏 ACCOMMODATION – for Hanningfield, contact the Tourist Information Centre in Chelmsford on 01245 283400, or Brentwood on 01277 200300. The centre in Waltham Abbey will be able to help with accommodation in the area around Walthamstow reservoirs. Phone them on 01992 652295.

RIB VALLEY FISHERY – HERTFORDSHIRE

This delightful, very thoughtfully-run fishery is made up of two lakes. Rib Valley, the original water, spreads to around twelve acres whilst the newer, smaller Millennium Lake covers about four. Both are spectacular waters, but the Millennium really catches the eye. It's so stunningly crystal clear that you wonder how you're ever going to get a trout out of it.

Indeed, in bright, clear conditions fish can be challenging, even though stocking levels are kept pretty high. The management suggests fishing with comparatively small flies and keeping on the move. Also, keep an eye open for fish circuiting the lake, often close in and frequently feeding hard. A nymph fished in front of them can work. But you'll get many a rejection and it's probably better to fish whatever fly you've got on very slowly indeed.

It's tempting to go down on leader diameter when conditions seem to make life impossible, but be wary. There are some very big fish in both Rib

Valley and Millennium and they fight spectacularly well. In fact, most locals advise against going beneath six or seven pound breaking strain.

As far as flies go, all the usual suspects feature. Take a few lures with you – not really the purest way but sometimes necessary to stir the aggression of a rainbow. Make sure you've got teams of buzzers and be prepared to fish nymphs pretty well static close to the bottom. Above all, take the advice of management and regulars because they really do know what they're talking about and they'll go out of their way to help you get a bend in your rod.

There's an enlightened approach to catch and release at Rib Valley, where it is encouraged providing water temperatures remain reasonably low. Catch and release is a thorny issue on many still waters and some anglers remain staunchly against it. In the Millennium Lake, it's so clear that you can see that it works: many fish are caught repeatedly, showing that they can go back without ill-effect – providing they're treated well and unhooked carefully.

There are some cracking fish at Rib Valley. The lake record stands at over eighteen pounds, but you'll find plenty of fish in the four- to eight-pound category and above... good-looking specimens that fight tremendously well. The little River Rib winds its way around the fishery and helps encourage the natural feel of the place. You can't help but feel a pang for the past when you see this tiny watercourse and remember how rivers such as the Rib, the Bean and the Minram were, not so long ago, glorious trout streams. Abstraction has tragically seen them off and it's to the credit of the new breed of fishery managers that we now have still waters to take their place.

⌃ **SEASON** – open all year round.

⚡ **TICKETS** – contact Richard Vigus at Westmill Farm, Ware, Herts on 01920 469290. Booking is important for the Millennium Lake. There is a whole range of price structures, the most expensive being £50 a day on Millennium Lake for a four-fish bag. However, Rib Valley is less expensive at £26 for four fish. There is a whole scale of charges for lower bag limits, half-day fishing, catch and release and so on. Boat hire is available on Rib Valley.

→ **DIRECTIONS** – the fishery lies off the A602 Ware/Stevenage road, half a mile from the A10 roundabout. You'll find it signposted on the left when you head north. There's a rough track past a garden centre into the valley, and you'll find the two lakes and lodge at the bottom of the hill.

⇥ **ACCOMMODATION** – the Tourist Information Centre in Hertford on 01992 584322 can advise on the various kinds of accommodation in the area.

NORTON FISHERY – ESSEX

Norton is another of these small fisheries that have sprung up in the Greater London area, providing a welcome amount of sport for resident Londoners and visitors alike.

Norton isn't a particularly old water but it's settled down nicely and is maturing well. The water certainly is in tiptop order. There are casting platforms around the lake, which don't add to a natural look but they are practical and well built and, combined with the really warm welcome you receive at Norton, make you feel that you're being looked after very well.

There's plenty of weed in the water and, if the sun is high, you get some pretty spectacular views through Polaroid glasses – especially of some of the very big fish that inhabit the lake. If you latch onto one of the over-wintered rainbows, for example, you're really in for a treat. Norton is a water that's crying out for surface fishing – buzzers, sedges, mayflies, hoppers, daddies and so on – but there are times when a slow sinking line with a damsel fly, for example, worked back just above the weed, will work wonders. Try something like this when the light is very bright and the fish are sulking. Careful catch and release is allowed, which I'm all for because it makes a challenge on a crystal clear water such as Norton all the more intriguing.

SEASON – open all year.

TICKETS – apply to Bert Norton or Jason Brown at Norton Fishery, Stapleford Tawny, Abridge, Essex on 01708 688445. Prices start at £30 a day with a whole range of prices beneath that for shorter durations. Boats are also available.

RECORDS – stocking is with very good-sized rainbows and the present record is 18lb plus.

DIRECTIONS – leave the M11 at junction 6 and take the A113 to Abridge. Turn left over the River Roding onto the B172, which is signposted Theydon Bois. Take the first right to Abridge golf course and eventually you will come to the fishery on your right.

ACCOMMODATION – the Tourist Information Centre in Brentwood on 01277 200300 will be able to give advice on accommodation in the area.

BRICKHOUSE FARM – ESSEX

Brickhouse is representative of the brave attempts to bring fly fishing right into the heart of the South East. Brickhouse is very close indeed to the M25 but it's in a truly rural location that gives it a real feel of serenity and charm. This is only a relatively small water but it's intimate and has a very fishy feel to it. Moreover, the fish come from the renowned Hanningfield's stock, so they're beautiful and really do put a bend in the rod.

The water is well stocked and you probably won't need to resort to anything particularly fancy. A floating line will probably do. If you want to go deeper, simply increase the length of your leader. A gold head nymph, Pheasant Tail or any one of the buzzer tribe will probably do for starters.

All in all, a pleasant little trout fishery with improving facilities.

☀ SEASON – open all year round.

⚡ TICKETS – contact Dennis Bean, Brickhouse Farm, Doddinghurst Road, Brentwood, Essex CM15 0SG on 07713 952999. There is a scale of ticket charges, rising to £20. Catch and release is available for members, and membership is reasonably priced.

→ DIRECTIONS – Brickhouse is just north of Brentwood. Leave the M25 at junction 28 and head along the A1023 towards Brentwood town centre. Take the A128 to Chipping Ongar. Turn right into Doddinghurst Road, which you'll find just before the Robin Hood pub. Drive under the A12 towards Doddinghurst, past a leisure centre. After about a mile, you will see the fishery well signposted. You'll find it down a track, past the farm.

⊨ ACCOMMODATION – information about various kinds of accommodation can be obtained from the Tourist Information Centre in Brentwood. Phone 01277 200300 for details.

CLAVERING LAKE – ESSEX

Clavering is hidden away deep in the heart of rural Essex. The M11 might roar close by, but you won't hear it... only horses' hooves trotting down the lane behind. There are two lakes at Clavering – one of around four acres, going down to about twelve feet, and another of around two acres offering depths to some fourteen feet. The lakes are set in very pleasant surroundings and hold splendidly-conditioned fish in gin-clear water.

There's an adventurous stocking policy at Clavering, with fish well in excess of double figures going in on a frequent basis. Look out for the excellent rainbows, browns, brookies and tigers. The average size of fish going in is well over two pounds, so you won't be disappointed.

One of the things that makes Clavering special is the quality of the winter fly fishing. Really good sport can be enjoyed on the top in the winter months, and daddies, for example, work well throughout the year. The only time that fish can prove difficult is during very hot summer periods, when they can get a bit sluggish. You can still take them off the surface if you show a little patience – they come very well to all manner of buzzers. Or perhaps put on an intermediate line and work a nymph very slowly down deep.

☀ SEASON – open all year.

⚡ TICKETS – here is a quite complicated system of charges – £25 allows you to fish for the day, take four fish and operate catch and release; £15 allows you simply to fish catch and release. Please note that fish over three pounds are not to be taken.

→ DIRECTIONS – take the B1038, which runs from Newport to Buntingford. Follow the road into Clavering and on a sharp left-hand bend you will see the Cricketers pub on the right. Turn right next to the pub, then take the first left. Follow the road for a mile until you see a green sign with the name 'Greenhall' on it. Turn right and continue until you see the lake. Purchase the tickets from the farmhouse, which is past the lake on the left.

⊨ ACCOMMODATION – details about various kinds of accommodation can be obtained from the Tourist Information Centre in Saffron Walden on 01799 510444.

❧ HIGHLY RECOMMENDED FISHERIES ❧

- *Felix Farm, Bracknell, Berks. Ten-acre fishery. Very well stocked with some big fish. Spring fed. Highly recommended.*
- *Woodchurch Trout Fishery, near Ashford, Kent. Phone 01233 860253 for details. Pleasant fishery with good-sized rainbows.*
- *Tenterden Trout Waters, Tenterden, Kent. Contact on 01580 763201. A lot of surface activity with good-sized fish.*
- *Yew Tree Trout Fishery, Rotherfield, East Sussex. Call for information on 01892 852430. Fishes well to dry flies and small buzzers on floating line. Pleasant fishery.*
- *Duncton Mill, Petworth, West Sussex. Call 01798 342048 for more information. Three lakes. Feeling of space. Nice fishery.*

Fly-Fishing Sites
in East Anglia

1. Grafham Water
2. Northbank Trout Fishery
3. Larkwood Trout Fishery
4. Whinburgh Trout Lakes
5. The River Wensum
6. Bure Valley Lakes

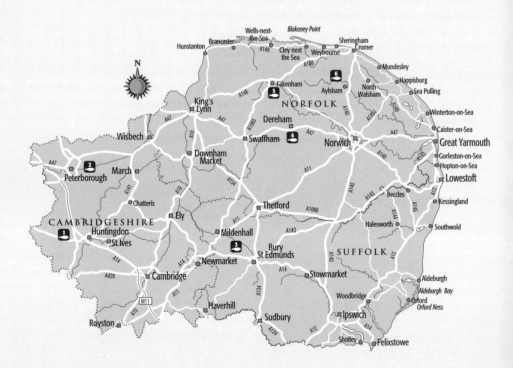

' *East Anglia is a bit underrated, I guess, when it comes to game fishing. Everybody seems to think solely of the coarse fishing in the region, which I agree is very good indeed. But there is water for the trout man and some of it's of high quality and relatively obtainable. Of course, we East Anglians do have Grafham Water, which is still one of the best reservoirs anywhere. And there are a number of really first-class commercial trout fisheries that have stood the test of time and gone from strength to strength. In Norfolk, especially, there are also some first-rate little trout streams. The problem for the visitor is that access is closely guarded. You do have the Wensum, though, in central Norfolk, which gives you a really good idea of what things are like. A real chalk stream this one is. And then, finally, you've got the unexpected. The North Norfolk coast, for example, is absolutely ideal for fly fishing for bass. It's generally sandy but with gently shelving gravel banks and the fish come in really close. My preference is for a floating line and a big streamer-type fly that resembles a sand eel. Providing you can get a fly out a bit of a way you've always got a chance. Watch out for small fish breaking the surface or gulls coming down for a feeding spree and you can be sure bass are somewhere close at hand. And who knows, you might also pick up one or two of the sea trout that also visit the area. All exciting stuff.* '

JOE REED, NATIONAL TRUST WARDEN OF THE NORTH NORFOLK COAST

And Joe is right, East Anglia offers a huge amount to the visitor and some of it you wouldn't suspect. A couple of the streams – the Nar and Wensum in particular – have stretches that are available to Salmon and Trout Association members. Phone 0207 2835838 for membership details. So when you're planning a family holiday with a trout rod also in mind, don't discount East Anglia: you could be surprised.

GRAFHAM WATER – CAMBRIDGESHIRE

Grafham Water is really one of the jewels of East Anglia – a historic trout water that continues to produce quite staggering catches of rainbows. In fact, 1999 was officially Grafham's best season ever – and that's saying something – with sixty percent of the trout caught weighing two pounds or more and a fishery record of eleven pounds twelve ounces.

In part, Grafham has always produced such excellent quality fish because of the high numbers of roach and bream fry that are spawned every season. These small fish allow the rainbows to pile on weight very quickly indeed, and the browns – some of them really huge fish – benefit particularly.

Grafham has a fleet of fifty boats – well-designed and very stable – and records seem to suggest that catches are higher afloat than from the bank. For those visitors who are a little unsure about boat fishing, courses are available from one of the experts who run the fishery lodge.

Grafham has always been a very appealing place to fish: lovely scenery, very high-quality rainbows and browns, and free-rising fish.

☀ ON THE RIVERBANK ☀

- *If you see numbers of fish dying or in distress you are probably witnessing a pollution incident. It's your responsibility to phone the Environment Agency (EA) emergency hotline (available twenty-four hours a day in England and Wales) on 0800 807060 immediately.*
- *The faster you act, the more likely it is that the incident can be controlled and dealt with. Contact club officials, too.*
- *When reporting incidents, ensure you give clear, concise details of what you have seen and good directions to the actual location of the incident.*
- *Take water samples if you can. These can provide the vital evidence needed to assist the EA in bringing a successful prosecution.*
- *If you have a camera with you, its useful to take photographs of what you are witnessing. This may also help in the prosecution process.*
- *Enjoy the countryside and respect its life and work.*
- *Fasten all gates.*
- *Keep to public footpaths across farmland.*
- *Take your litter home.*
- *Help to keep all water clean.*
- *Protect wildlife, plants and trees.*

ÏBlack and green flies have often seemed to do very well at Grafham, certainly for the very big fish. So, bearing that in mind, try a Viva or even a Green Pea. These work well on floating lines, sometimes with a long leader if conditions are still and bright. Don't overlook buzzer fishing for much of the year – you'd be surprised just how many big fish fall to these tiny flies in the surface film.

SEASON – Grafham opens on 1 April and runs through to 31 December.

TICKETS – phone the fishery's lodge on 01480 810531 to book a bank or boat permit. A day ticket is £17 (eight-fish limit), a late afternoon/evening ticket is £12 and a morning ticket is £10 (both four-fish limit). A two-man boat costs £24 a day and £13 for the evening.

RECORDS – brown trout 19lbs 12oz and rainbow trout 13lbs 13oz.

RULES – do ensure that you obtain a fishery map before setting out. There is no fishing close to the bird hides or around the nature reserve.

DIRECTIONS – Grafham Water can be accessed from the A14 to Grafham village or from the A1 to Buckden. The various access points are well signposted.

ACCOMMODATION – the Tourist Information Centre in Cambridge on 01223 322640 can supply details of various kinds of accommodation in the area.

NORTHBANK TROUT FISHERY – CAMBRIDGESHIRE

Northbank really is a superb trout fishery – pretty, remote and beautifully cared for. It is one of those places that give you a huge amount of faith in the commercial trout fishery. It's a comparatively large water at around sixteen acres or so, with a large island that also increases the amount of bank space available. In fact, given the two together, there's well over a mile of fishing on offer. It's not a particularly deep water, with holes going to around sixteen feet or so, but this hardly matters – especially as the water is so clear and the dry fly works so well.

This is a point emphasised by one of the bailiffs, Clyde Anthony: 'Northbank is an absolutely superb dry-fly fishery, partly because it's so crystal clear. We open in March and I go dry fly from the word go. I use small flies early season and then get bigger as conditions dictate. All the usual patterns work – Black and Peacock Spider, for example, or gold-ribbed Hare's Ear. Later on in the summer you can't beat a Daddy's. Fish the water carefully and slowly. It's the same when the fish are fry feeding towards the back end. All manner of Victors and Butchers work well, but once again, don't drag them back at ninety miles an hour. If you want a bit of guidance, I'm always willing to advise'.

That's the hallmark of this attractive, friendly fishery: you never really feel you're on your own at Northbank – there's always somebody willing to help out. A really great fishery in a lost, lonely part of the world.

⛵ **SEASON** – Northbank is open from 6 March to 24 October, and the lake opens from 7.00am and closes at dusk.

🎣 **TICKETS** – contact the owner John Cutteridge at Northbank Trout Fishery, Northbank, Thorney, Peterborough, Cambridgeshire, PE6 0RP. Tickets for four hours cost £7, allowing you to take one fish and then move on to catch and release. For two fish taken, you pay £10. An all-day ticket with one fish taken is £9, with two fish £12 and with four fish taken £18. Catch and release is available thereafter.

📷 **RECORDS** – the lake is stocked with both browns and rainbows from one and a quarter pounds upwards but with plenty of far bigger fish. The lake record is 15lbs 2oz with many fish of 5lbs and above.

➡️ **DIRECTIONS** – take the A47 towards Peterborough turning down the B1040 signposted to Whittlesey. In three and a half to four miles, you will come to the Dog in Doublet Bridge with lock gates over the River Nene. Turn right at the bridge along the road following the Nene. You will see signs to the fishery on the right-hand side.

🛏️ **ACCOMMODATION** – try Wisteria House, Church Lane, Peterborough, PE6 7DT on 01733 252272 or contact the Tourist Information Centre in Peterborough on 01733 452336.

LARKWOOD TROUT FISHERY – SUFFOLK

Larkwood Fishery, created just over fifteen years ago, goes from strength to strength. There are two lakes at Larkwood – Glebe Lake and West Stow – both about three acres and featuring shallows and depths down to about twenty feet. Both waters are very pretty and totally matured, surrounded by trees and good reed growth. Providing the weather does not become too warm, both lakes remain clear and there is a profusion of natural life. Look out for alder fly larva, pea mussels, shrimps, snails, beetle larva of all kinds, corixa and damsel fly nymphs. It's on a diet as rich and varied as this that the rainbow and brown trout grow very quickly to become superb fish.

The fishery is run by an expert angler, Ian McGregor, an entertaining Scot who offers an outstandingly warm welcome. Ian stocks with fish of about a pound and a quarter to a pound and a half minimum. However, there are plenty of fish much bigger than that into the seven- to eight-pound bracket and above. Ian stocks every other day so there's a constant top up of fresh fish. 'Virtually all my regulars here use nothing but a floating line', says Ian.

'If the fish are down deep, then they'll use a long leader and obviously if they're up on the surface you can go that bit shorter. And you don't need many different fly patterns here. Providing you've got some damsels, Hare's Ears, some Pheasant Tails and Cats Whiskers then you should really do okay.'

Larkwood is open all the year round and fishes particularly well in the winter when it's still possible to take fish – very well-mended rainbows indeed – on nymphs as well as lures. Larkwood is highly recommended, especially in an area where there isn't a huge amount of competition – not that that means Ian is going to relax his standards.

☼ **Season** – open all year round.

✦ **Tickets** – contact Ian McGregor on 01284 728612 at Larkwood Fishery, West Stow, Bury St Edmunds, Suffolk. Permits cost £17 for four fish and £10 for two fish. It is possible to practise catch and release before you've taken your limit.

➡ **Directions** – from Bury St Edmunds, take the A1101 towards Mildenhall. Turn right at the West Stow signpost and follow this road down past the country park. The fishery is one mile further along the road, situated on the right.

➥ **Accommodation** – phone the local Tourist Information Centre in Bury St Edmunds on 01284 764667 for advice on various kinds of accommodation in the area.

WHINBURGH TROUT LAKES – NORFOLK

There really are some idyllic commercial trout fisheries available now all over the country, and Whinburgh, deep in the heart of Norfolk, is one of the nicest. Whinburgh comprises two lakes joined in the middle and set in beautiful, mature, landscaped grounds. There's easy access for wheelchairs, along with a brew-up shed. Wives and friends who aren't fishing are more than welcome… providing they're well-behaved, says owner Mr Potter!

Whinburgh is a fertile, sheltered water with both browns and rainbows, generally between one and ten pounds in weight. It lends itself to dry fly fishing, as it only averages six feet deep and the water is often very clear.

Overall, Whinburgh is a very lovely, very friendly place to fish, and the trout, which are in excellent condition, offer a satisfying challenge without ever appearing too diabolically difficult! Highly recommended.

☼ **Season** – Whinburgh is open all year round and there is a competition once a month.

✦ **Tickets** – contact Whinburgh Trout Lake, Dereham NR19 1QU for up-to-the-minute ticket information. At the time of writing, day tickets are £12.50 for nine hours on a catch and release basis. Half-day tickets (five hours) cost £7.50. Concessions are made for anglers aged 65 plus on Tuesday, Wednesday and Thursday.

RECORDS – the biggest rainbow has clocked in at over 13lb and double-figure browns have been seen, if not landed.

RULES – Whinburgh is based on catch and release so barbless hooks are mandatory. It is permitted to kill rainbows and these cost £1.75 per pound to take.

→ **DIRECTIONS** – Whinburgh is situated on the B1135 between Dereham and Wymondham.

ACCOMMODATION – there are a number of bed and breakfast guesthouses in the area and the Tourist Information Centre in Dereham will be able to supply details. Phone them on 01362 698992.

❧ YOUR RESPONSIBILITIES ❧

As an angler it's important that you support the bodies that fight for the sport you love. These organisations cannot operate without the help of fishermen… and very frequently pathetically small numbers join the most worthwhile of organisations.

- *The Atlantic Salmon Trust, on 01796 473439, fights tooth and nail for the welfare of salmon both in home waters and in the high seas.*
- *The Salmon and Trout Association not only provides good local fishing for members but also works very hard indeed to ensure stable habitats. You can contact the Association on 020 7283 5838.*
- *The Wild Trout Society publishes an excellent magazine for its members and also promotes the wild brown trout fishing of this country. The address is 92-104 Carnwarth Road, London SW6 3HW.*
- *The Grayling Society fights directly for one of our most beautiful freshwater fish that is frequently under pressure. To join, contact Mike Tebbs, Ayott Lodge, 38 The Crescent, Belmont, Sutton, Surrey SM2 6BJ.*
- *The Anglers Conservation Association has been fighting polluters for over half a century. Its list of court successes is extraordinary. Join this if you join nothing else, by contacting the Association on 0118 971 4770.*

THE RIVER WENSUM – NORFOLK

The Wensum up until fifty years ago was an unsung delight. It runs over chalk, is largely spring-fed and for many centuries in its life was at least the equivalent of many of the Hampshire streams. Then agriculture took over. The river was, tragically, dredged. The water table fell, the glistening gravel rapids became clogged with silt, and fish stocks – especially of trout and grayling – began to plummet.

However, all is not lost. The Environment Agency has instituted sweeping changes along the river system. Fakenham Angling Club is also a very progressive body and, wherever possible, has devoted itself to bettering the trout fishing. So, today, the upper River Wensum is absolutely worth a visit.

Fakenham Angling Club controls some two to three miles of top quality river trout fishing in the vicinity of Fakenham itself. Here you can wander, almost always alone, through lovely farmland and fish a gin-clear river. In places it's deep. There are pools. There arc dancing shallows. You'll come across dace, perhaps roach, and you'll see the odd pike. It's that type of mixed river but the brown trout fishing can be excellent. I say brown trout because Fakenham only stock browns and will have no truck with rainbows. So, you see, the spirit of the old Wensum is being kept alive nicely.

Stalk your fish very carefully. The water is clear and these fish become very wild indeed. It's quite possible that some of them truly are wild, because a certain amount of natural breeding does still take place today. Nymphs of all sorts work well – especially leaded ones in the deeper water, which runs over luxuriant weed beds. There is something of a mayfly hatch and, for the dry fly fisherman, there are rises most evenings during warmer periods.

So, okay, this might not be quite the style of trout fishing that you'd find on some of the Hampshire streams but it's not far behind and, for the low cost, I don't think you'd find much better anywhere.

SEASON – 1 April to 30 October, though the best of the fishing is from later in the spring to the early autumn.

TICKETS – Fakenham Angling Club sells tickets from Dave's Fishing Tackle, Miller's Walk, Fakenham. Phone 01328 862543 for details. It pays to phone in advance because a limited number of day tickets are issued. Also, note that there are no day tickets on Sundays.

DIRECTIONS – The Wensum rises just to the west of Fakenham and flows south east, more or less parallel to the A1067 to Norwich.

ACCOMMODATION – why not try Sculthorpe Mill, close to Fakenham, on 01328 856161 right at the head of the fishing itself? This is a delightfully converted old water mill that provides excellent accommodation and food.

BURE VALLEY LAKES – NORFOLK

Bure Valley Fisheries offers some wonderfully secluded trout fishing in a fold of North Norfolk countryside well away from maddening civilisation. Moreover, the fishery is run with huge intelligence by Mike Smith, its owner. Catch and release on the fifteen-acre lake is encouraged, although rainbows can be taken at a cost of £1.80 a pound. Interestingly, Mike says that at least eighty percent of fish are returned. This means that he does not have to rely overly on stocked fish, and the condition and wariness of the resident rainbows continually increases. In fact, regulars say there is not a still-water trout fishery to touch it in the whole of East Anglia.

There is more to come, as the name of the fishery implies. The upper River Bure winds alongside the lake and is an absolute delight to fish for those who appreciate the charm of small, wild brown trout. These fish are not particularly large – six to eight ounces is the norm – but what they lack in size they make up for in cunning, beauty and fighting ability on light tackle. The river abounds with features and this is really creepy-crawly stuff to flick your fly into miniature pools and riffles.

Most excitingly of all, the infant Bure has a startlingly rich mayfly hatch that takes place in very late May and early June. The mayflies tend to dribble off through most of the daylight hours, which gives the trout fisherman a real chance of some spectacular sport. All browns must be returned at once and the fishing is available over six generously laid-out beats.

SEASON – the lake is open all the year round and the river fishing begins on 1 April and ends on the last day of October.

TICKETS – the trout lakes cost £12.50 for a full day, £10 for six hours and £7.50 for an evening ticket. The river costs £12.50 per day, per beat. All fishing is catch and release, though rainbows can be taken for £1.80 per pound.

RECORDS – 9lb exactly for a wild brown trout and 12lb 6oz for rainbows. As the lake is stocked with fish to fifteen pounds plus, this record must surely be smashed shortly.

DIRECTIONS – Take the A140 from Norwich to Aylsham, then the B1354 to Saxthorpe. The fishery is on the right-hand side, four miles out of Aylsham. You will find it down a mile long cart track.

ACCOMMODATION – contact the Tourist Information Centre in Cromer on 01263 512497 or at North Walsham on 01263 721070. They will advise on local accommodation.

☆ HIGHLY RECOMMENDED FISHERIES ☆

- *Earith Lakes, Cambridgeshire. Call 01487 740301 for further information. Really big fish in lovely condition. Highly recommended.*
- *Narborough Trout Farm, Nr. King's Lynn, Norfolk, phone 01760 338005. Four lakes and a stream. Very long established fishery with an historic big fish reputation.*

FLY-FISHING SITES IN THE MIDLANDS

1. Ladybower Reservoir
2. The Derbyshire Rivers
3. Yeaveley Trout Fishery
4. Gailey Trout Fishery
5. Loynton Hall
6. Packington Fisheries
7. Ravensthorpe
8. Eyebrook

9. Rutland Water
10. Pitsford Water
11. Draycote Water
12. Salford Trout Lakes
13. Farmoor Trout Fishery

'You know John, these Midland reservoirs came at just the right time for me in many ways. I'd started out as a coarse fisherman and done very well with pike and tench and all the usual species, but I was looking for a new challenge. Then, suddenly, all these extraordinary venues burst upon the fishing scene, and as a young man I realised I could be in at the beginnings of it all. Exciting stuff. Everybody was learning. New rods, new reels, new flies and new methods.'

Bob Church, England fly-fishing international (in an interview in 1988)

The Midlands, especially Northamptonshire, will always be remembered as the home of British reservoir trout fishing techniques. This side of the sport took off in the 1960s: greater affluence, increasing car transport and improving tackle standards all meant that game fishing began to look attractive to anglers who had previously only fished coarse. The large reservoirs around the Midlands, created to supply domestic and industrial needs, cried out to be stocked, and the results were frequently spectacular. Grafham in Cambridgeshire led the way. When the fishing was opened here, the trout that had been stocked were found to have put on weight dramatically and traditional fly-fishing gear was rendered useless. The same at Rutland, Eyebrook, Draycote and a host of other waters.

In response to the demands of these big reservoirs and savage trout, new rods, reels and techniques were developed by such legendary masters of the Northamptonshire reservoir school as Dick Shrive, Arthur Cove and Bob Church. The Midlands' reservoirs are now a vital part of the game-fishing scene and, thanks to men like Church, you can now enjoy them with tackle and techniques that have been honed to perfection. These are great waters and the fish can be really stunning. Ticket prices are generally very reasonable and helpful fishery staff will make your visit as enjoyable and fruitful as possible.

THE MIDLANDS

LADYBOWER RESERVOIR – DERBYSHIRE

I caught my very first trout on a fly at lovely Ladybower Reservoir many, many years ago, and for that reason alone I retain huge affection for the water. But it's always a joy to go back to Ladybower, perched high in the Peak District National Park, enjoying stunning views over an amazingly mountainous landscape. Ladybower is wild, lonesome fishing and you'd hardly believe you're a mere dozen or so miles west of Sheffield when you're out there, either on the water or enjoying the thirteen miles of virtually untrodden bankside.

The stocking policies are very generous, and each year over thirty-five thousand mixed browns and rainbows are stocked – including browns to over four pounds and rainbows to ten pounds plus. And these are wonderful fish, nearly all of them raised carefully at the fishery itself under expert care.

Hiring a boat probably gives you the best chance of a bumper bag of fish but Ladybower is about more than this. I prefer to travel light and walk as many miles of the bank as I feel up to during the day. Imitative patterns can succeed at Ladybower, but most locals tend to go for more traditional reservoir flies like the Ace of Spades, the Orange Chenille and Viva. There are times, however, especially late in the summer, when fish will come to the surface quite avidly and dry fly fishing can pay dividends both early and late. One bonus with such a large water is that much of the marginal path is largely untrodden during the day and even big fish will come in very close indeed. So take your time, stalk carefully and you could be in for quite a surprise.

☀ SEASON – Ladybower opens on 6 March and closes on 13 October.

✦ TICKETS – tickets are available from the Fishery Office, Ladybower Reservoir, Ashopton Road, Bamford, Derbyshire S33 0AZ on 01433 651254. Day tickets cost £12.50 for the full day and £8.60 for an afternoon/evening ticket. Boats, with or without electric outboards, are also bookable through the Fishery Office. Tuition is available with prior booking through the Fishery Office.

🛆 RECORDS – rainbow trout 17lb 4oz, brown trout 11lb 7oz.

➔ DIRECTIONS – the reservoir is well-signposted off the A6013, ten miles west of Sheffield.

⊨ ACCOMMODATION – Bamford, a short distance from the reservoir, boasts several good hotels – try the Ladybower Inn on 01433 651241, the Yorkshire Bridge Inn on 01433 651361, the Marquis of Granby on 01433 651206 and the Rising Sun on 01433 651323. The Tourist Information Centre in Sheffield on 0114 221 1900 will also be able to advise on further accommodation.

The Derbyshire Jewels –
The Rivers Derwent, Wye and Dove

These three rivers, although surrounded by some of the biggest industrial centres of the north, offer some of the most superb fly fishing in the entire country. Mind you, because these waters are so prolific and beautiful and because they are so close to large urban areas, the pressure on them is great, and day tickets are not easy to come by. However, for the visitor, there are opportunities and they are very well worth pursuing indeed. For me, personally, the Derwent is at its best at Baslow along the Chatsworth fishery, which is available to residents of the Cavendish Hotel. There are several miles of beautiful water here and the trout fishing can be just extraordinary. Perhaps even more special is the grayling fishing, especially in the Christmas holiday period when there is a festive spirit in the hotel and the nearby market towns. Fly fishing can be wonderful, but bait fishing is also allowed and some of the very best water is found directly in front of the hall itself, just a little upriver of the imposing bridge.

The Wye is equally prolific and ticket availability exists on the Haddon Hall estate, close to Bakewell. The fishing here can be second to none, and the river is fascinating to read – a snake of meanders, deep pools and enticing ripples. Once again, grayling are present and can grow very large indeed, but it's probably the wild-bred rainbows that excite the most. Yes, wild-bred… these stunning fish are like miniature steelheads and have looks and battling qualities you'll remember the rest of your days.

Now we come to what is perhaps the jewel in the crown, the River Dove, the enchanting stream made famous in *The Compleat Angler* by Izaak Walton and his collaborator, Cotton. Trout and grayling waters don't come any more beautiful than this, and the pinnacle of northern fly fishing can be seen in Dovedale itself. Just the walk itself is breathtaking. Of course, it is a walker's paradise, but if you can get out early or late you can almost sense the presence of Walton at your shoulder.

Once again, the trout fishing is quite, quite superb and on a summer evening, fishing the dry fly, you'd think you were in paradise. Imagine this: a small, characterful, crystal-clear river, winding between dramatic hills, overhung with forest. But, again, once the frosts begin to bite and the leaves fall, the grayling come into their own – and what grayling these are. Two-pounders are not uncommon and threes exist, lurking in the deep, mysterious pools.

Season – generally, the waters are available for trout from the beginning of April until early October but it is as well to check on local restrictions. Grayling fishing on most of the waters continues throughout the winter, closing on 14 March.

❧ RESERVOIR TIPS (THE MIDLANDS) ❧

Reservoirs can appear very daunting on first view, especially if you've been used to a small, commercial-type fishery. However, the benefits of reservoir fishing are immense.

- *Location is obviously a key. Don't get too entrenched, rather keep on the move until you contact fish. Remember rainbows especially are shoal fish and where you get one take, you're likely to get more.*
- *Binoculars are a good idea to spot surface activity up or down the bank. Look for rising fish, fry feeding fish and fish feeding just sub-surface.*
- *Where it's permitted, it's tempting to wade out from the bank a little way to get nearer to fish rising just beyond your casting capabilities. Remember, however, that all you're likely to do is push the fish even further away from the bank, and so little is achieved. You also run the risk of scaring fish that are willing to feed close in.*
- *If your casting is a problem to you, the chances are you need to either learn or brush up on your double haul techniques. You'll find that casting clinics are available at some of the big Midland reservoirs or, alternatively, you could get yourself down to the Sportfish fly fishing school at Reading. Phone 0118 9303860 for more details.*
- *Don't be afraid to experiment. If you've been a lure fisherman all your life, by all means start out with this technique but don't be afraid to switch over to nymphs, buzzers or even dry flies if you think they'd serve you better. You'll be amazed how quickly you pick up new techniques.*
- *A boat can work wonders on large waters. Always wear buoyancy aids and, if you're a little unsure about taking to the waves, go out a few times with somebody experienced. That way your confidence will build up and you'll begin to appreciate the advantages boat fishing can give.*
- *Reservoir experts often take a whole team of sinkers but, for a start, I'd suggest an intermediate line with a sink rate of between one and a half and two and a half inches per second. This way you can count your lines down and get an idea of the depths your flies are fishing at.*
- *If you've been used to lure fishing, don't forget that you can fish nymphs, buzzers, very, very slowly. Indeed, fishing them static is more and more common. Of course, they're not totally immobile because there'll always be some drift but these techniques work the flies in the gentlest of ways.*
- *Above all, don't be afraid to ask advice of other anglers and, especially, the fishery staff. Almost invariably they will prove to be hugely helpful and very generous with their time and advice.*

✦ TICKETS – the head river keeper on the Haddon Estate, Mr Ross, is of great help both for tickets on the Derwent and the Wye. Contact him on 01629 636255. Two-day tickets for the Derwent are also available from the Peacock Hotel, Rowsley, on 01629 733518, both to residents and non-residents. The other possibility on the Derwent is the Cavendish water. Phone the Cavendish Hotel on 01246 582311 for full details. You have to be resident at the hotel, which is not cheap, but, believe me, the experience is one that lasts. As for the Wye, Mr Ross will give full information. The Dove can be fished by guests of the Izaak Walton Hotel, Yeaveley Estate, Nr. Ashbourne. Phone 01335 350555 for information. There is also a small trout lake available – perfect for beginners. The tackle shop, Foster's of Ashbourne Ltd., Compton Bridge, Ashbourne DE6 1BX is also a fund of information and publishes a local guide to day-ticket waters. Try also Stephen Moores on 01629 640159 for day tickets on the Monsal Dale Fishery.

➡ DIRECTIONS – it is best to apply to the various ticket sources for directions to these waters. Be careful not to stray over beat boundaries.

🛏 ACCOMMODATION – the hotels mentioned are all excellent. There is also a good deal of bed and breakfast accommodation in this popular holiday area. Contact Mr & Mrs Beltney, Congreave Farm, Congreave, Stanton in the Peak, Derbyshire DE4 2NF. The Tourist Information Centres at Ashbourne, on 01335 343666, and Bakewell, on 01629 813227, will also be able to give advice about accommodation.

YEAVELEY TROUT FISHERY – DERBYSHIRE

I've included Yeaveley for several reasons. Although it is only a small water, it does provide something of an antidote to the larger reservoirs found all around the Midlands. At times it's just nice to go intimate. Secondly, I've frequently been happy to use Yeaveley in the autumn and winter when I've initially wanted to fish for grayling in the surrounding rivers but found them totally out of condition and in flood. A day spent on Yeaveley has been a very happy substitute. And thirdly, Yeaveley is a really spectacularly attractive and challenging little fishery in its own right.

It's only around one and a quarter acres or so but is now around ten years old and has matured magnificently. There are good levels of cover that allow for successful stalking (if you're good enough) on a water that is always crystal clear. Two springs account for this and also help to promote a very active fly life on the water.

Depths aren't great – around fifteen feet maximum – so it's quite possible to fish the year round with a floating line or, at most, an intermediate. Yeaveley is a spectacular dry fly water; on the phone with the owner once I was told that a fourteen-pound rainbow had actually come off the surface, and that was in late October. Buzzers work well the year round, especially very small ones on a size sixteen or even an eighteen. In fact, stay small whatever flies you decide to use.

And go barbless. Yeaveley operates a very progressive ticket system. You can take your first three fish and then operate on catch and release thereafter, to what is considered a sportsman-like limit. That's around ten fish or so in the eyes of the fishery owner, and who would quibble at that? Quite sensibly, too, he suggests not taking fish of over three and a half pounds.

You're afforded a very warm welcome at Yeaveley. There's a welcoming cabin, a pub close by, and tuition can also be arranged. And, with the sight of ten-pound-plus rainbows cruising in the clear water at my feet, I don't find it too hard to give up on my grayling fishing for the day!

☼ **SEASON** – open all year apart from Christmas Day.

↬ **TICKETS** – contact Yeaveley Estate and Trout Fishery, Yeaveley, Nr. Ashbourne, Derbyshire, on 01335 330247, www.yeaveley-estate.co.uk. Tickets cost £22 per day. The first three fish are taken, and catch and release thereafter. Barbless hooks please.

➔ **DIRECTIONS** – take the A515 south from Ashbourne for about two miles. You'll find the village of Yeaveley signposted on the left. Follow the road into the village and you will see the Horseshoe pub on the right. This is next to the driveway to the fishery, which is well signposted.

⊨ **ACCOMMODATION** – the Tourist Information Centre in Ashbourne, on 01335 343666, will be able to supply information on various kinds of accommodation in the area. Ashbourne has a wealth of hotels and bed and breakfast accommodation.

GAILEY TROUT FISHERY – STAFFORDSHIRE

Gailey is well worth a look for many reasons. Firstly, it is situated just off the M6 and couldn't be easier to find. Secondly, at thirty-eight acres it gives a nice impression of space and variety. You never really feel crowded on the water, especially if you book one of the reasonably-priced boats and get out behind one of the islands.

Gailey is also renowned as a top water, and throughout most of the year dry flies and buzzers on a floating line are pretty much all you'll need. Mind you, as autumn develops, the bigger trout, particularly, begin to fry feed with a vengeance. The water is kept very well stocked and if you don't succeed down at the deeper dam end where the water is around seventeen feet, you can try stalking up in the shallows where you'll find three feet or less. Stocking policies are not only generous, but fish sizes, too, are impressive. The smallest fish that you will come across are around a pound and a half but there is a generous quota of double-figure fish. There are browns, rainbows, spectacular tigers and a few brook trout.

I ought to make mention of the pike fishing. From the first Sunday in November you might well be sharing the water with some keen predator men. Mind you, although we're talking about big pike here with many going over twenty-five and even thirty pounds, they don't really interfere with the trout fishing at all. Fish of this size simply take one big fish every week or so and then lie pretty well dormant. There was a problem with jack pike but the management have sorted this out. Research over the last fifteen or twenty years has proved that providing you keep the big pike in the water, the jacks will have a very hard time of it and trout fishing will benefit. Out of interest, the pike fishing costs £7.50 a day and £1 is retained, put in a kitty and paid out at the end of the season to the angler with the biggest recorded specimen!

A very attractive, very well-stocked fishery and highly recommended.

SEASON – open throughout the year. The fishery opens at 8.00am and closes at dusk.

TICKETS – contact Gailey Trout Fishery, Gailey Lea Lane, Gailey, Stafford ST1P 5PT, or phone 01785 715848 for details. A day ticket costs £40 and allows a four-fish limit with catch and release thereafter. A half-day ticket costs £15, with a three-fish limit and catch and release afterwards. There is also a very enlightened junior special ticket that costs £10 and allows under-sixteens to take one fish, with catch and release after that. Sporting tickets cost £15 for the day, or £10 for OAPs.

DIRECTIONS – on the M6, take junction 12 and the A5 towards Cannock. Take the first turning on the left and you will come to the fishery entrance. This is a cul-de-sac with a canal at the end so you can't go far wrong!

ACCOMMODATION – the Tourist Information Centre in Stafford, on 01785 610619, can give advice on suitable accommodation in the area.

LOYNTON HALL – STAFFORDSHIRE

Loynton Hall has deservedly built up a tremendous reputation in this part of the country. There are three lakes, all set in stunning countryside and all very well stocked. The water goes down to forty feet in places and can colour up after heavy rain. All this means that floating lines can and do work, but don't neglect to bring along a sinker – especially in the summer when the water is warmer and the fish can go down deep.

The rainbows are stunning... they're put in at a minimum of two pounds, but – and this is the exciting thing – they do go up to thirty pounds with lots of twenties. In fact, regular visitors can easily get a dozen or more doubles during the course of a season. There are also some very good browns as well, but please note that all browns caught must be released.

There aren't really any specific tips for Loynton Hall – the fishery owners say that most of the locals do best by keeping on the move, and it's best to experiment freely with flies, depths, retrieves and so on until a winning formula for the day is found. What's made quite clear is that this is not a stocky-bashing water. Loynton really is a place to take seriously. Mind you, the welcome is very warm indeed and it's such a beautiful place with big fish that the whole package is very difficult to resist.

⛅ **SEASON** – open all year round. The fishery opens at 8.00am Saturday and Sunday and 9.00am Friday (closed Monday-Thursday). It's quite an early closing fishery and shuts down at 8.00pm, even in the summer.

🪰 **TICKETS** – contact Steve Masters at Loynton Hall Trout Fishery, Nr. Woodseaves, Staffordshire on 01785 284261. A six-fish day ticket is £40, a five-fish day ticket is £35, a four-fish day ticket £30, a three-fish, eight-hour ticket £25 and a two-fish, six-hour ticket £20. You can take your quota and then move on to catch and release, but do this very carefully indeed. There are also five sporting tickets each day priced at £10 for six hours or all day for £15.

➡ **DIRECTIONS** – you'll find Loynton Hall north of Telbury on the A519, between Newport and Eccleshall. Loynton Hall is very well signposted in the little village of Woodseaves.

🛏 **ACCOMMODATION** – contact the Tourist Information Centre in Stafford, on 01785 619619, for details of accommodation in this area.

PACKINGTON FISHERIES – WARWICKSHIRE

No wonder Packington is so massively popular amongst Midland anglers, situated as it is between Birmingham and Coventry and yet in its own placid, countryside setting. Packington has built up a tremendous reputation over the years as a place offering a wide variety of sport over three day-ticket lakes, all generously stocked with high quality, good-sized fish.

There are three lakes at Packington open to the day-ticket fisherman. Broadwater and Cocks Close lakes are both into the teens of acres. Cocks Close is almost invariably very clear, whereas Broadwater does colour up after rain. There is also six-acre Burnetiron, the smallest of the three waters but the one open for catch and release methods.

Damsel fly patterns are probably the most reliable, year-round fish catchers at Packington, but the water fishes very well for nymphs and buzzers throughout the warmer months, epoxy buzzers being particularly recommended. As the water cools, lures like Appetisers and Cat's Whiskers come into their own, but don't be tempted to fish them too quickly .

Packington is within the hurly-burly of the Midlands but you really wouldn't know it and so if you do find yourself in the area and you fancy catching beautifully conditioned trout from one and a half to ten pounds or more, give this enchanting fishery a few hours of your time.

☀ SEASON – open all the year apart from Christmas Day, Boxing Day and New Year's Day.

✦ TICKETS – contact Packington Fisheries, Broadwater, Maxstoke Lane, Meriden, Nr. Coventry CV7 7HR on 01676 522754. Day-ticket prices vary: a £16 ticket entitles you to two fish or, at the top of the scale, a £24 ticket that allows you five fish. Evening tickets (from 4pm) cost £12. There is catch and release on one lake, Burnetiron, at £14.

→ DIRECTIONS – take the A45 from Coventry towards Birmingham. You will find Packington Fisheries just before the M42 on the right-hand side. Turn down Shepherds Lane right next to the Forest of Arden Hotel.

⊨ ACCOMMODATION – the Forest of Arden is highly recommended. For further information contact the Tourist Information Centre in Coventry on 02476 227264.

RAVENSTHORPE – NORTHAMPTONSHIRE

Ravensthorpe is a comparatively small reservoir, set in rolling middle-English countryside. There are many exciting things about Ravensthorpe. One of them is the catch and release policy that allows anglers to carry on fishing way beyond their two-fish bag limit. Ravensthorpe's other claim to fame is float tubing – a form of fishing in which you climb into something that looks like a cross between a frogman's outfit and a rubber tyre. It really is the way to get close to your fish and all the necessary equipment is available for hire at £10 a day or £6 for half a day, including tuition.

Less adventurous fishermen might also try one of the fleet of boats with an electric outboard – a really excellent tool for gliding you in close to rising fish. This is a lovely, friendly, smaller water where the visiting angler is instantly welcomed and made to feel at home. Lovely fish and a lovely setting – who could ask for more?

☀ SEASON – 26 February to 31 December.

✦ TICKETS – these are £17 for a day, or £12 for a half day tickets. Catch and release tickets are £14. Boats start at £12 a day, £10 for an evening, for a single occupant. Phone 01604 781350 and speak to the Senior Warden at the Pitsford Lodge for full details.

⚖ RECORDS – brown trout 14lb, rainbow trout 12lb 6oz.

→ **DIRECTIONS** – Ravensthorpe is situated very close to the M1/M6 junction and is well signposted.

⊨ **ACCOMMODATION** – information about suitable accommodation can be obtained from the Tourist Information Centre in Northampton on 01604 622677.

EYEBROOK – LEICESTERSHIRE

Reservoirs can have character, be beautiful and possess a charming individuality. This is what Eyebrook proves. Perhaps it's something to do with its age: it's an old, mature reservoir and has offered fly fishing for just on sixty-five years. Perhaps it's something to do with its coziness. Eyebrook is 'only' four hundred acres, and this makes it manageable, even to a newcomer. There are still five miles of very good bank fishing available and all of them are easily accessible by quiet, picturesque country lanes.

This is a lovely water, nestling amongst the rolling hills of the Welland valley. It's a little like a lowland loch and you only have to half close your eyes to feel the remoteness. This setting makes it important as a Site of Special Scientific Interest, and as a focus of local wildlife groups. Anglers, please remember this aspect when you're fishing and take special care not to leave litter or nylon.

Fishing at Eyebrook is nearly always productive. That's partly because there is a lot of good, top-water action from trout that are both high in quality and numbers. New stock is added weekly and Eyebrook now has around thirty-five thousand trout in its reservoir.

My own personal favourite at Eyebrook is to get afloat: naturally, a boat gives you advantages of access, especially when, like Eyebrook itself, the boats are modern and well-maintained. The feeling of loneliness that Eyebrook induces is also enhanced when you're out on your own on the water.

Lures work well early season when the waters are cold, but as conditions warm, nymphs and buzzers take over. Although depths are frequently over twenty feet, a floating line is generally sufficient once that chill goes off the reservoir. Late season sport can be excellent with daddies and shrimp and corixa imitations. Remember, Eyebrook is a fertile reservoir and the well-conditioned trout are used to a natural larder. All in all, highly recommended.

SEASON – The reservoir is open between 30 March and 24 October, from 7.00am until one hour after sunset.

TICKETS – these are available at the reservoir. Contact the Fishing Lodge, Eyebrook

It's a privilege to be in Dovedale as the winter sun seeks to break the horizon. Mists hang across the peaks, the landscape is washed with subtle colours and the river flows through a pewter world.

The River Usk exerts a magnetic hold on those that fish it regularly. It offers excellent trout and grayling opportunities, and the salmon populations are holding up well.

Bait fishing for salmon is practised less and less, and perhaps rightly so as a bait-caught fish is more difficult to release. Nonetheless, controlling a worm or a prawn in fast water takes some skill.

There are many small rivers for the fly fisherman throughout the British Isles. They all demand a cautious approach and delicate pinpoint casting.

*Cenarth Falls are legendary for Welsh sea trout fishing – enchanting by day, impelling by night.
Big sea trout continue to make their way up these falls as they have done for centuries.*

Reservoir, Great Eastern Road, Caldecott, Leicestershire on 01536 770264. A day ticket costs £16, an afternoon ticket £10 and an evening one £8. There are two wheely boats, for the use of the disabled, which cost £8, and fifteen motorboats at £16.

➜ **DIRECTIONS** – You will find Eyebrook off the A47 between Leicester and Peterborough. At Uppingham, take the A6003 south to Caldecott. Then follow the AA signs to the reservoir.

✚ **EXTRA INFORMATION** – Eyebrook sports an excellent modern fishing lodge with disabled facilities. There is also a specialist mobile tackle shop at the reservoir each weekend and there are always flies and leaders on sale at the lodge.

▬ **ACCOMMODATION** – the Tourist Information Centre in Leicester on 0116 299 8888 will be able to advise on suitable accommodation.

RUTLAND WATER – LEICESTERSHIRE

Rutland Water offers three thousand, one hundred acres of some of Europe's best trout fishing. Set in lovely rolling countryside, a day at Rutland is always a pleasure for the rawest novice and the most experienced international match angler. On a water as large as Rutland, it makes real sense to get local knowledge, and the fishery staff here really are welcoming and experienced. Nigel Savage, Nathan Clayton and the rest of the Rutland team are enthusiasts who fish the water themselves regularly. As they like to say, they know their fishing, they understand their water better than anyone – and they have years of experience in helping others to enjoy their sport.

Just a word about Rutland in the autumn and early winter. More and more anglers are finding that, brilliant though the summer sport is, as the year begins to wane the quality of the fish themselves becomes outstanding.

Many of the very big fish are caught on fry imitations – not surprising, considering the millions of coarse fish fingerlings that inhabit the water. However, by the late summer, insect hatches are extravagant and dry flies and buzzer fishing in the surface film can produce some excellent fishing. The best brown of all in 2005 – 11lb – was caught off the bank using a floating line and a small diawl bach!

There's a great deal of sensitivity in the rules and regulations at Rutland, and boat and bank anglers can opt for catch and release. This was introduced for anglers who want to continue fishing beyond any bag limit, but also for those who simply want to practise their technique and those who just don't like the idea of killing their fish.

Facilities at Rutland are excellent, with a fully-equipped tackle shop offering everything the angler might need. There is a large and well-maintained fleet of sixty-five powered boats, and the fishing lodge is the place to glean information and reasonably-priced food and drink. Another great idea is the introduction of a special low-priced one fish permit for beginners who can also hire tackle inexpensively from the lodge. Courses are run, and individual tuition is available for anglers of all standards. So, if on holiday, you can really make this a family day out.

⚒ **SEASON** – the fishery opens between 1 April and 31 December.

⚓ **TICKETS** – for bookings, contact Rutland Water Fishery Lodge, Rutland Water South Shore, Normanton Car Park, Edith Weston, Oakham, Rutland LE15 8HD, or phone the fishery lodge on 01780 686441 for their scale of charges. For example, a standard day ticket costs £17 (eight-fish limit) and a morning ticket costs £12 (four-fish limit). Full day boat hire is £24, half day £15. The tackle shop can be contacted on 01780 686443. There is also a twenty-four-hour weather line on 09063 610206.

⚖ **RECORDS** – 14lb 12oz and 13lb 8oz for brown trout and rainbow respectively.

🐟 **RULES** – do obey fishery rules and avoid nature reserves and bird watching centres.

➡ **DIRECTIONS** – Rutland Water is found very close to the town of Uppingham on the A47 from Leicester. It is well-signposted.

🛏 **ACCOMMODATION** – try the White Hart, Uppingham, on 01572 822229. Or phone Rutland Water Angling Breaks on 01572 723004 quoting booking reference ANG 1901. Try also The Exeter Arms, Barrowden, Rutland, on 01572 747247; The Old Rectory, Belton, Nr. Uppingham, on 01572 717279; or The Horse and Jockey, Manton, on 01572 737335. For a B & B, contact Little Hoo Bed and Breakfast on 01780 460293. Try also the Tourist Information Centre in Leicester on 0116 299 8888.

PITSFORD WATER – NORTHAMPTONSHIRE

Pitsford lies in lovely, wooded countryside next to the Brixworth Country Park. Being so close to Northampton, its situation attracts nature lovers and anglers alike, so remember that you are an ambassador for our sport. Indeed, co-operation is very much the spirit at Pitsford, and the lovely lodge that blends in so well with its surroundings is a centre for both anglers and nature reserve wardens.

Pitsford is all about education and the environment. There is a schoolroom in the lodge where techniques can be brushed up on. To encourage newcomers, the management also offers cheaper day and boat tickets. So, in theory, you and your family can learn to fish and then go out onto the water and put what you have learnt into practice – and all for a very modest charge. This, surely, is very much the caring face of fishing in the future. Naturally enough, there is also a catch and release policy, and the water is made available for pike fishing on certain weekends of the year.

Everyone, therefore is catered for, and, as an angler, please be aware that some parts of the fishery are out of bounds at certain times of the year. This is done very much for the good of the wildlife, and it doesn't do the fish any harm either to have some sort of sanctuary.

There is a range of tickets available, so please enquire when booking. Pitsford is also now open well into December, so it's worthwhile just having a quick thought about some tips for late autumn and the really cold months. You will find that there will be fly hatches, especially after Indian summers, on most reservoirs until the frosts become really cruel. For this reason you can still fish a floating line and a team of buzzers. But remember to fish them slowly, ideally in a crosswind, so that they swing around gently in an arc. You'll find that fish are quite happy to come into the shallows at this time of the year, especially early and late in the day, and, as the fishing is visual, you won't have any problems detecting takes.

It's tempting to think that you'll need a sinking line to get down deep for coldwater fish, but this certainly isn't always the case and floaters or intermediates are generally all you'll need. Remember that you'll probably have to work your flies more slowly than you do in the summer and for this reason a floater with a long leader gives you perfect control. You'll find that fish are still roaming quite freely, although their pace will probably have slowed down. It's only after a very hard frost that they won't be near the surface and you'll probably have to count your intermediate line down.

Don't discount the first few hours of the afternoon in the winter. The water is probably at its warmest between noon and about 3.00pm, especially if there's any sun. The fish are very likely to respond. And you may not find any great advantage in going out in a boat once the weather really cools down. Remember that winter fishing is all about that slow retrieve I've talked about, and this is frequently more easily achieved from the bank. Don't bother fishing into the teeth of an icy wind. Wrap up well in warm, watertight clothing, and break the day up with two or three visits back to the lodge for coffee and a chat. If the fishing is a little difficult, it's amazing how confidence rises after a few minutes' fishing talk.

SEASON – 17 March to 31 December.
TICKETS – Pitsford Water, Pitsford Lodge, Brixworth Road, Holcot NN6 9SJ. Bookings can be made on 01604 781350.
DIRECTIONS – take the A508 north from Northampton towards Market Harborough. Pitsford Reservoir is on the right-hand side in a few miles. It will be signed along with the Brixworth Country Park.
ACCOMMODATION – the Tourist Information Centre in Northampton, on 01604 622677, will be able to supply details of accommodation in the area.

DRAYCOTE WATER – WARWICKSHIRE

As fishery manager Keith Causer explains, Draycote has been an excellent buzzer water for the last two or three years. For large parts of the season, buzzers on floating lines have been all that any angler has needed to take the excellently conditioned browns and rainbows from Draycote.

Draycote is a big reservoir and, at six hundred acres, it often attracts quite a breeze. If you are fishing a team of buzzers, it can be difficult to get a line out, especially with a long leader and the wind blowing directly into your face. If you're having trouble trying to straighten your leader, try to cast 'under the wind', as they say. If you're fishing a long leader, make sure your heaviest fly, perhaps a damsel fly nymph or something similar, is on the point. This will help turn the whole team over nicely. Also, remember that casting a long leader involves having more line out than the length of the leader itself. Unless you do this, you just can't get casting. If you want to fish very close into the bank, therefore, what you're going to have to do is simply stand further back from the water to get everything in action. As an added bonus… the fish are less likely to see you.

The average weight at Draycote tends to be around two pounds for both browns and rainbows, but the fish grow on excellently – in the 2000 season, browns to over thirteen pounds were taken and rainbows just a little lighter.

SEASON – open April to October inclusive. The fishery opens at 7.30am and closes one hour after dusk.

TICKETS – contact Draycote Water, Kites Hardwick, Rugby, Warwickshire, CV23 8AB, on 01788 812018. An £18.50 day ticket allows you to take eight fish and a £10.50 ticket after 3.00pm allows you to take five fish. You are allowed to catch and release fish until you've actually killed your limit, then you must cease fishing. There are twenty-five motorboats available at £20.50 per day. Three people are allowed in the boat, but only two may fish because of safety reasons. Rowing boats are £12 a day.

DIRECTIONS – Draycote is found off the A426 south of Rugby. Cross the M45 and you will see it signposted shortly after on the right.

ACCOMMODATION – try Judy Slater, The Orchards, Kites Hardwick, Rugby, Warwickshire, on 01926 812621. The Tourist Information Centre in Rugby, on 01788 534970, will be able to advise on other suitable accommodation.

SALFORD TROUT LAKES – OXFORDSHIRE

Salford was a water unknown to me until a recent fishing trip to Wales when it was highly recommended by one of my companions. Salford's reputation isn't particularly built on massive rainbows and as my companion said, 'You won't find the fishmongers there!' No, Salford is

more about quiet serenity, fascinating fishing and beautiful surroundings. Two lovely lakes make up the fishery, both with islands, and neither particularly deep – nine feet is around about the maximum. That means that floating lines and buzzers are a pretty good way to start. Mind you, dry flies and damsels all work too. That's the pleasurable part about Salford – imitative patterns are just all the rage!

A good fish at Salford is three or four pounds and the fishery record, a rainbow, is only about eight pounds. But does that matter? This is a guidebook, not one on angling ethics, but perhaps we've become a little too obsessed with size over the last twenty-five years or so. Perhaps size is just a macho thing or something to do with the trophy mentality. You won't need any of that at Salford – just an appreciation of beautiful waters and a very genuine, warm welcome and atmosphere.

☀ **SEASON** – Salford Trout Lakes are closed from the end of October to mid March.
🎟 **TICKETS** – contact Salford Trout Lakes, Salford, Chipping Norton, Oxfordshire, OX7 5YZ or phone or fax 01608 643209. Day tickets cost £25 for four fish. A half-day ticket costs £17 and entitles you to two fish. For more information, see www.salfordtroutlakes.co.uk.
➡ **DIRECTIONS** – from Chipping Norton, north-west of Oxford, take the A44 Evesham road. After a mile, take the right-hand road to Salford. At the T-junction, turn right, then left. Follow this road for about half a mile and you will see a farm track signposted Rectory Farm and Trout Lakes on the left.
🛏 **ACCOMMODATION** – details of accommodation can be obtained from the Tourist Information Centres in Chipping Norton on 01608 644379 and Oxford on 01865 726871. There are also bed and breakfast facilities at Rectory Farm itself. Also, contact South Coombe Lodge Guesthouse, The Bungalow, Chipping Norton, Oxfordshire, on 01608 643068. Or, Swan Lodge, Oxford Road, Chipping Norton, Oxfordshire, on 01608 678736.

FARMOOR TROUT FISHERY – OXFORDSHIRE

Farmoor, at around about two hundred and forty acres, has long been a stamping ground for Oxfordshire trout fishermen. Although it's pretty much a concrete bowl, the stocking levels are high and the challenge is great. And, reputedly, Farmoor trout fight like tigers.

From the bank, play around with buzzers and nymphs, especially in the warmer months. Strike indicators are firm favourites with the locals and these mean that the most delicate takes can be seen and struck at. The other advantage of a strike indicator is that you can set your flies to work at a predetermined depth, and this can be very useful on days when they're being very picky.

When the water is high, you'll find that the trout will come in close, in just three to five feet of water, but if the water level is lower, you'll probably find them further out and deeper down. A standard leader between ten and fifteen feet in length is enough for most conditions, but if you're not getting takes, then a twenty-foot leader can make all the difference. The whole point is to fish sensitively and thoughtfully and keep experimenting with flies, depths and retrieves until you begin to pick up fish. In the winter, the Booby seems to take over, especially as there's deep water close in. Fish the fly very slowly with a figure of eight retrieve, or even let it hang static.

Farmoor operates a catch and kill policy when fishing from the bank – it's simply that too many trout were landed, allowed to bounce on the stones and then were returned in a dying condition. This is a particular shame when you think that the browns and rainbows are only stocked at one to two pounds in Farmoor but quickly grow on to double-figure size. Fine fish like this have to be respected. Catch and release is possible from a boat providing sporting ethics are upheld. Barbless hooks, nymphs and imitative flies and, if possible, unhooking in the water all help to preserve stocks.

SEASON – Farmoor opens in mid March and runs until the end of January. The fishery opens at 10.30am and closes at dusk.

TICKETS – contact Farmoor Trout Fishery, Cumnor Road, Farmoor, Oxford OX2 9NS on 01865 863033. From the bank, an eight-fish limit costs £16 and a four-fish limit £13. There is a two fish evening ticket that covers the last three hours of the day for £7.50. A motorboat costs £8 for one person and £10 for two people. Ordinary ticket prices apply on top. From the boat, you can also buy a one-man sporting ticket for £20 or a two-man sporting ticket for £25. All fish are returned.

DIRECTIONS – from Oxford, take the A40 towards Cheltenham. In three miles or so, turn left onto the B4044. Cross the toll bridge, which costs five pence! In Farmoor village, turn right onto the B017. In three quarters of a mile you will find the reservoir on the right-hand side. Look out for the brown sign.

ACCOMMODATION – contact the Tourist Information Centre in Oxford, on 01865 726871, who can supply information on various kinds of accommodation available in the area.

❖ HIGHLY RECOMMENDED FISHERIES ❖

- *Santhill Trout Fishery, Bourton-on-the-Water, Gloucestershire. Phone 01451 810291. Beautiful twenty-six-acre lake. Very rich. Imitative patterns work well. Closed January and February.*
- *Elinor Trout Fishery, Nr. Aldwincle, Northants. For details, phone 01832 720786. Fifty-acre gravel pit. Well matured. Big rainbows and browns. Good challenge.*
- *Churchill Fishery, Mursley, Bucks. Pretty, well-stocked lake. Nice lodge. Feeling of exclusivity.*

FLY-FISHING SITES IN WALES

1. Anglesey
2. The River Dee
3. Gwernan Lake
4. Tal-y-Llyn Fisheries
5. The River Irfon
6. The Rivers Nevern & Teifi
7. White House Mill Fishery
8. The River Towy
9. Glyncorrwg Ponds
10. Ravensnest
11. The River Usk

'When I first came to Wales, like everybody else I'd heard
of the famous sea trout rivers like the Teifi or the Conway,
and knew there were some really excellent brown trout lakes
like Bala and Vyrnwy. I also knew that the Wye had been
the foremost salmon river in England or Wales, and that the
Usk wasn't far behind it. But it was only after I'd lived here
for a few years that I began to appreciate what tremendous
potential for the game fisherman is hidden under the surface.
The point about Wales is that for every famous game fishery,
there are twenty forgotten or undiscovered ones. For example,
you'll find mountain streams and hidden hill lakes full of
wild browns. Or, you can find small west coast spate rivers
that can produce unexpectedly large sea trout. Even salmon.
There are pools everywhere tucked into mountainsides
where you can enjoy excellent rainbow trout fishing,
and in the all but unknown tributaries of the Wye
you'll find some of the best grayling fishing anywhere
in Europe. There are so many grayling in central Wales
of such a large size with no-one fishing for them that
I almost feel I'm king of my own private paradise.'

PETER SMITH, WRITER, HOTELIER AND ADVISOR TO THE WELSH TOURIST BOARD

And Peter even missed out chub, dace and pike from some
of the crystal rivers, and even bass and mullet from many
of the estuaries... all well within the scope of the fly fisherman.
You can drive east to west or north to south, criss-crossing
Wales however you like, and I honestly doubt if you'll go ten
miles without finding your own little fly-fishing paradise.

Much of the water is controlled by local clubs and it's often
possible to pick up a season's membership for a very low fee,
especially considering the standard of the fishing. Alternatively,
hotels also control many lengths of river and you can nearly
always find somebody to point you in the right direction.

FLY FISHING ON ANGLESEY

This lovely island offers some extraordinarily fine and unexpected fly fishing to the visitor. Moreover, the whole pace of life here – especially away from the coast – is easy, ambling and you can wind down to the flow of nature in the way that every successful game angler should.

Game fishing on the island is dominated by three waters – Llyn Alaw, Llyn Cefni and Llyn Coron – all three of which are beautiful, well-stocked and available to the visiting angler. Llyn Alaw is the largest, covering nearly eight hundred acres, and is in the centre of north Anglesey. It's a shallow, fertile water and lies among rolling, open pasture land. A brisk wind can make fly casting difficult at times, but the lake has many bays and headlands that offer possible fishing opportunities whichever direction the wind blows in. The reservoir is a haven for wildlife, and supports a variety of breeding birds throughout the summer. You will find common terns at the eastern shallow end of the reservoir, which has been designated a nature reserve.

Llyn Cefni is a quarter the size of Alaw and again is found in central Anglesey. The water is fringed by conifer plantations, although areas have been felled to give more light and a greater feeling of space. There are two interconnected lakes divided by a disused railway line and, marvellously, there is still a large population of naturally spawning brown trout.

Llyn Coron is a shallow, rich seventy-acre lake lying at the inland end of the Aberffraw dune system and this gives it a really unique character.

⇒ A FEW WORDS TO THE WISE ⇐

Just a few advisory words about fishing in Wales:
- *Do be careful with the beats on some of these Welsh rivers and streams as they're not always very clearly marked and you can unwittingly end up poaching – an embarrassing situation that you need to avoid.*
- *The weather in the wilder parts of Wales can change dramatically. Even on an apparently warm, summer morning it pays to stick a waterproof in your bag if you're going to be out for any length of time.*
- *Take special care on the bigger lakes and reservoirs as a wind can easily spring up out of seemingly nowhere.*
- *A final word of warning: if you're thinking of pursuing those upper Wye grayling that Peter talks about, then avoid the annual Royal Welsh Show that's based in Builth Wells… you'll find the roads a nightmare and accommodation impossible to come by.*

Llyn Coron supports a good stock of brown trout and, excitingly, some sea trout have also been caught in the lake after running up the River Ffraw during the summer months. In short, these waters really provide a huge resource for the visiting fly fisherman and between them, offer something for everyone.

LLYN ALAW

SEASON – rainbow and brown trout seasons run from March to October. Call to confirm exact dates.

TICKETS AND RULES – permits are available from the Llyn Alaw visitors' centre, which can be contacted by phone on 01407 730762. Six fish are allowed per permit. Note that spinning and worm fishing is also allowed on this reservoir so you might not be alone! Day tickets cost £14 and evening tickets £12. One-week tickets cost £70. Concessions available. Boats are also for hire, but it pays to book in advance.

→ DIRECTIONS – travel along the A5 and turn right at the signpost for Llanerchymedd/Trefor. Go along this road until you reach a crossroads. Turn left and take the next right. Follow the brown signs until the end of the road. Turn right, then right again at the next brown sign.

LLYN CEFNI

SEASON – you can fish from 20 March to 17 October for all trout, both browns and rainbows. A thousand brown trout are stocked at the start of the season and rainbows are put in as the season progresses.

RECORDS – The record catch is 7lb for a brown trout and 6lb for a rainbow.

TICKETS AND RULES – tickets can be bought from Tackle and Guns Shop, Menai Bridge, or Pete Rowe Jewellers, Llangefni. You can also direct enquiries to the Honorary Secretary, G. R. Williams, Tyn Lon, Pentre Perw, Gaerwen, Anglesey. There is a bag limit of six fish per permit and the size limit is ten inches. Day tickets are £14, evening tickets (from 4.00pm) are £10 and weekly tickets are £45.

→ DIRECTIONS – take the A5 express way along Anglesey to Llangefni. Then take the B5109 towards Bodffordd. After about two miles turn right, signposted Welsh Water Cefni Treatment Works.

LLYN CORON

SEASON – 20 March to 17 October.

PERMITS AND RULES – permits are actually issued on the lake itself but for more information phone either 01407 840253 or the Bailiff, Cliff Girling, on 01407 810801. Day tickets cost £10 and the catch limit is four fish per day.

→ DIRECTIONS – follow the A5 onto the island and through the village of Gaerwen. Go past two right turnings signposted Llangefni, take the next left, signposted Aberffraw. Turn left towards Llangadwaladr, and follow signs over the bridge. Before the village of Aberffrad and the bridge, take a right turn. Follow the track to the lakes.

WELSH GRAYLING

Wales offers an intriguing mix of all manner of fishing types. There are large reservoirs, enchanting sea trout rivers, beautifully run stocked commercial fisheries and major, internationally famous rivers such as the Usk with, at times, important runs of salmon. But there are all sorts of hidden excitements in between, the sort of fishing you'd hardly ever guess at. One of my own personal favourites is the Welsh grayling. Of course, I'm not saying that Welsh grayling are any different to Scottish grayling or English grayling, but there's something about Wales that makes them treasured, as though they're hidden, tucked into folds in the hills.

I have two favourite grayling rivers in Wales so let's start to the north on the Welsh Dee, around that charming little town of Llangollen. Llangollen Angling Association has twelve miles of bank fishing around the town and it's all accessible and very grayling-rich. Of course there are trout too – some splendid fish running to three pounds or so – but it's the grayling that makes the water truly special. Try deep-fished Czech nymphs in some of the major pools or steadier glides. Believe me, there are really big grayling swimming here in the most charming of waters. Every yard cries out to be explored.

Let's move now to the delightful River Irfon, in mid Wales, centred in the county of Powys. The Irfon treks its dancing way through some of the most wonderful, secret Welsh countryside. Once again, there are plenty of trout – beautiful wild browns – and reasonable runs of salmon later in the year, but for me, it's the grayling that win the vote. Like the Dee, there are some very big fish, beautifully proportioned and coloured, probably averaging a pound to a pound and a half. Again, you will find that they come freely to all manner of nymphs and goldheads – especially fished reasonably deep. There's a real beauty to fishing these waters for their grayling: It's as though it's your secret, an area the rest of the world has overlooked.

☼ SEASON – the grayling is classed as a coarse fish and so its closed season is from 14 March to 16 June. However, it's wise to check with the contact numbers that fishing is allowed after the trout season ends in October.

THE DEE
✦ TICKETS – permits are obtainable from Hughes Newsagents, 12 Chapel Street, Llangollen, Denbighshire, LL20 8NN. They can be contacted on 01978 860155.
→ DIRECTIONS – Llangollen lies on the A5 as you travel west from Chirk, which is on the A5/A483 Oswestry to Wrexham road.
⊨ ACCOMMODATION – Llangollen is a bustling holiday town with many bed and breakfasts, guesthouses and hotels. Check out the Royal Hotel on 01978 860202; their bedrooms actually overlook the river.

THE IRFON

✠ ⊨ TICKETS AND ACCOMMODATION – up river at Llangammarch Wells, the Lake Country House Hotel LD4 4BS has around five miles of the Irfon and day tickets are sometimes offered to non-residents, although this is a spectacular place to stay. Phone 01591 620202 for details. Down river we come to some splendid water at Builth Wells, where the River Irfon joins its parent, the River Wye. The place to go here is the Caer Beris Manor Hotel, Builth Wells, Powys, LD2 3MP. The hotel has rods on the water running through its own delightful grounds and can also arrange tickets on nearby stretches of the Wye. Phone 01982 552601 for more information. There is also an enchanting stocked rainbow trout water just across from the hotel over the Indiana Jones-type suspension bridge. This is truly delightful fishing and if you find the groups of grayling you are truly in for an excellent day. The contact name here is Peter Smith, an Englishman but a long-term resident in Wales who knows absolutely everything about the fishing hereabouts and is a fund of knowledge and generosity.

⇒ SIGHT INDICATORS ⇐

Sight indicators are a little like floats in coarse fishing, in so far as they aid detection of a take. There are anglers who dislike them and regard them as unethical, but many think that in the right place they are totally legitimate, enhance enjoyment and increase sport.

- *Before even considering putting one on the line, always check with the fishery to see whether sight indicators can be used.*
- *Sight indicators are very useful indeed if you're dead drifting a nymph, say, in a stream for a winter grayling or before the wind in a reservoir.*
- *The sight indicator tends to act as a float, so adjust it until the flies beneath it are fishing the depth that you want.*
- *Always make sure that the sight indicator shows up brightly against the water that you're fishing. Reds and yellows are favourite colours.*
- *Don't make the sight indicator too big and heavy for the job.*
- *There are all manner of different sight indicator materials on the market. My favourites tend to be little polystyrene balls. Experiment until you find the kind of indicator pattern that works for you.*
- *Try different shapes. A marble-shaped indicator provides necessary buoyancy in fast water. If bites are delicate, try a longer, thinner shape.*
- *You don't always have to wait for the sight indicator to go beneath the surface. Strike if it holds up momentarily or moves against the current.*
- *Remember that the sight indicator puts extra weight on your line, so you'll need to punch out your cast a little harder, especially into a wind.*

GWERNAN LAKE – GWYNEDD

Gwernan is a beautiful water set in the shadow of Cader Idris. This eleven-acre water is generally crystal clear with a maximum depth of around fifty feet and numerous deep holes providing shelter for the fish during very hot weather conditions. But there's more for the angler than the fish at Gwernan. With full SSSI status, the lake is patrolled by buzzards and red kites and there's a real feeling of peace and seclusion. Fishing is from any one of the Gwernan Lake Hotel's boats. This allows you to have good access to the fish, close to the lily and reed beds – natural magnets for the fish.

There are plenty of wild browns; the owners ask you to return these even though they grow to around four pounds in weight. Most of the rainbows are stocked between one and a half and two pounds but they grow very rapidly to six or seven pounds, and they fight extraordinarily well in this crystal-clear water. Small imitative patterns are very successful here. It's perfect for those that like to fish near the surface with dry flies and buzzers. If you're going down deeper, try spider, shrimp and nymph patterns.

In short, Gwernan is a perfect place to fish in seclusion with astonishing scenery and wildlife all around.

SEASON – the water is open all year round apart from Christmas Day.

TICKETS – phone Gwernan Lake Hotel on 01341 422488 or write to the hotel at Cader Road, Dolgellau, Gwynedd. £17.50 entitles you to a boat and a four-fish limit. An evening boat costs £10.

DIRECTIONS – from Dolgellau, take the Cader road south-west from the town. Take a left turn to the hotel just before a Shell garage on the right-hand side. Follow this road up towards Cader Idris itself. The lake and the hotel are on the right, approximately two miles from the centre of the town.

ACCOMMODATION – the Gwernan Lake Hotel itself offers very comfortable and reasonably priced accommodation. Bed and breakfast starts at £22.50 per head. There is also extensive bed and breakfast, guesthouse and hotel accommodation in Dolgellau itself. Contact the Tourist Information Centre in Dolgellau on 01341 422888 for further information. The Wales Tourist Board, Brunel House, 2 Fitzalan Road, Cardiff CF24 0UY can also offer advice.

78

Tal-y-Llyn Fisheries – Gwynedd

Tal-y-Llyn Lake is set in spectacular mountain scenery beneath the southern slopes of Cader Idris on the head waters of the Afon Dysynni. It's a shallow but very productive lake, just over two hundred acres in extent, and provides some of the finest brown trout fishing in Wales. Later on in the season, there is also a run of sea trout and salmon up the river and these can provide excellent and unexpected sport.

It's generally considered that April to June is the best period for brown trout when dapping and fly fishing can both present a very rewarding challenge. Throughout most of the season, however, Tal-y-Llyn has a famous hatch of olives, and imitative fly patterns are highly recommended.

This is a very beautiful water and the fishing is of the highest standard, so it is quite popular. Advance booking is advisable, especially for the boats, which are fully equipped with petrol engines and lifejackets. There's also a fishery shop that stocks a whole range of tackle.

 Season – 1 April to 17 October. The fishery is open from 9.00am until dusk.

 Tickets – a full day charge is £17 and a part-day, £12. Boat hire (with engine) is £20 for the full day and £14 for half a day. For enquiries, phone the fishery office on 01654 782282.

 Rules – artificial fly only from the bank or from a drifting boat. Natural fly may be used when dapping. No fishing when anchored up. Trolling, spinning and bait fishing are prohibited. No brown trout must be taken less than twelve inches, measured from the tip of the nose to the fork of the tail, and no more than four in a single day. Catch and release, using barbless hooks, is increasingly appreciated. All anglers must submit a return of catch, including a nil return, to the fishery office.

 Directions – Tal-y-Llyn is well-served by a number of primary roads including the A470 Cardiff to Llandudno road, the A487 from south-west Wales, the A494 to Chester and Merseyside and the A458 to Shrewsbury, connecting with the M54 and M6 for easy access, especially for the Midlands. The lake itself lies on the B4405, west of the A487 between Dolgellau and Machynlleth.

 Accommodation – anglers really cannot do better than stay at the Tynycornel Hotel. This old and picturesque hotel is right on the shores of the lake and is geared up for the needs of the fishermen. The hotel also has its own boats. For more details, phone 01654 782282 or send a fax on 01654 782679.

 Additional Fishing – Tal-y-Llyn Fisheries also control the fishing on Llyn Bugeilyn, a moorland lake set high up in the hills. This very beautiful water provides excellent small, wild brown trout fishing with no additional stocking. It's wisely considered important to maintain the wild nature of this extraordinary little fishery. Phone the fishery for details.

PEMBROKESHIRE RIVERS

Pembrokeshire is such a wonderful county that it's not surprising that its four major rivers are so appealing. These are the eastern Cleddau, the western Cleddau, the Nevern and the Lower Teifi – all of them mixed game fisheries running through stunning countryside. The first three are comparatively small, intimate rivers where a certain amount of stalking and careful casting is called for. They are principally sea and brown trout waters with only the occasional salmon showing. The Teifi can be a fine salmon river and, its devotees would argue, it's the best mixed game fish river in either England or Wales. However, the quality of the sea trout fishing in all the rivers can be high and ten-pound fish are far from uncommon. And you'd be surprised at the quality of the brown trout fishing as well.

All four are spate rivers and fine down quickly after rain. In fact, a good flush out generally leads to an influx of fish. But get a move on – after only a few hours the rivers run crystal clear again, winding their way through bleached beaches of gravel. If the water is low, you'll find salmon and the bigger sea trout lurking in the deep pools, especially the undercut banks.

The fining down period for salmon is the real taking time, especially later on in the season when more and more fish are progressing up to their spawning grounds. Traditionally, night-time will see the sea trout anglers abroad, searching their way through the darkness, listening for the sound of moving fish, plopping after insects or forcing their way up the shallows. Mind you, more anglers are experimenting with sea trout fishing during the daytime, perhaps using smaller flies on lighter leaders. Certainly, enough are caught during daylight hours to justify further experiments. The other bonus of daytime fishing is that the beauty of this lovely countryside – so much of it wooded – can really be absorbed. Fish are important but, let's remember, they're not everything and it's possible to enjoy the fishing here whatever the final tally.

☀ SEASON – the best time for sea trout is from late May to early September, and for salmon from August until October. The brown trout season runs from 1 April until 31 October.

🎣 TICKETS – the River Nevern is largely private but Nevern Angling Association controls six miles of some of the best fishing. Day tickets are very reasonably priced at £10 and available from the Trewern Arms, Nevern; The Reel Thing, Lower Market, Cardigan; and from Castaways, Cardigan. Enquiries can be addressed to Mrs Nika Pritchard on 01239 820671. The Nevern Angling Association also owns a stretch of the

Teifi – see above for ticket details – and the Teifi Trout Association has control of twenty miles of water between Cardigan and Newcastle Emlyn. This includes the famous Cenarth Falls stretch, which is extraordinarily scenic and prolific. Day tickets at £20 are available from The Reel Thing in Cardigan; Cenarth Falls Holiday Park; The Salmon Leap Inn, Cenarth; and the Afon Teifi Caravan Park in Pentrecagal. For the eastern Cleddau, tickets can be obtained from T. and P.J. Murphy on 01437 563604. For the western Cleddau, contact County Sports, 3 Old Bridge, Haverfordwest, who have day tickets available for £10 a day.

⊨ ACCOMMODATION – Pembrokeshire is a very popular tourist area, and the county's Tourist Board offers a holiday guide packed with the best accommodation available, from country house hotels to seaside cottage hideaways. Phone the Pembroke Visitors' Centre on 01646 622388 for copies.

WHITE HOUSE MILL FISHERY – DYFED

One of the more acclaimed still waters of Wales is definitely White House Mill, and over the years it's built up a reputation for producing some splendidly conditioned fish. The lake is very picturesque, surrounded by unspoilt farmland in the beautiful Marlais valley. It's not a huge water but there's a great deal of variety to its contours, and depths range between four feet in the margins to nineteen feet in the northern corner. But the thing that makes White House Mill so spectacular is the amount of natural food. It has a near-perfect pH of 7.4 and obtains a quarter of a million gallons a day from the nearby River Cwm. All this results in a heavy weed growth that heaves with shrimps, beetles, corixa... you name it.

The fishing here is very civilised and the owners quite rightly like to see anglers using floating lines, nymphs, dry flies. In short, go imitative and not flash. The fish deserve this: they over-winter beautifully and you're always in with a chance of a stunning fish or two – both rainbow and brown. True, in this crystal, fertile water the fish are not easy – especially as the owners allow a certain amount of catch and release for the regulars, so some of the biggest fish have seen it all before. In all, White House Mill is a really marvellous experience, big fish in a superb water, and you can't ask for more than that.

☀ SEASON – open all year.
🎣 TICKETS – for permits, phone 01834 831304. Or write to White House Mill, Lampeter Velfry, Whitland, Pembrokeshire. Tickets cost £10 for a two-fish limit. Thereafter, you pay £5 per fish, with a six-fish limit. You pay for the fish at the end of the day.
🚹 FACILITIES – tackle hire is available in the very pleasant lodge. There are some platforms and a couple of anglers' shelters.

81

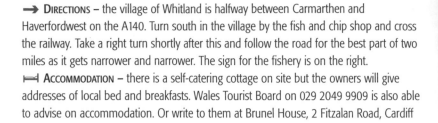

→ **DIRECTIONS** – the village of Whitland is halfway between Carmarthen and Haverfordwest on the A140. Turn south in the village by the fish and chip shop and cross the railway. Take a right turn shortly after this and follow the road for the best part of two miles as it gets narrower and narrower. The sign for the fishery is on the right.

⊨ **ACCOMMODATION** – there is a self-catering cottage on site but the owners will give addresses of local bed and breakfasts. Wales Tourist Board on 029 2049 9909 is also able to advise on accommodation. Or write to them at Brunel House, 2 Fitzalan Road, Cardiff CF24 0UY. A brochure giving details of accommodation and other information about Pembrokeshire is available by phoning 08705 103103.

THE RIVER TOWY

One of the most fertile of all the principality's rivers is the Towy with its main tributary the Cothi. The source of the seventy-five-mile-long Towy is in the Cambrian Mountains of mid-Wales and it has long been recognised as the best sea trout fishery in Britain, possibly in all of western Europe. If there is a national fish of Wales, then it's the sea trout. At its best, the Towy can provide shattering sport. Runs have declined in recent years, in common with most waters, but it's still an outstanding fishery, and individual specimens of eight pounds and over are caught most months. These are really fast growing fish and the largest ones enter the river in March and April, with the sizes gradually declining through the summer. The numbers of three- to six-pound fish running the river at this time can be phenomenal. Fresh-run sea trout continue to enter the river during September, but many of the fish that have come up earlier are turning gravid and should be left alone.

The Towy valley is a magical place, and to wander its banks as the ducks are coming in is a wonderful experience, especially when the fish are on the move and you can hear them powering through the pools and even scuttering up the rapids. All the traditional flies and methods will work here, but for added excitement try a big moth pattern, skating it back under the far bank branches.

While most people will still want to fish the water at night, there can be times when fishing small flies in the day can also be productive. Try a quite heavily weighted nymph and cast it to fish that you can see: you tend to find that they'll either vacate the area immediately or you'll get an instant take. It can be exciting stuff!

One important tip... do not come to a new river at dusk and expect to be able to fish it competently. Instead, spend the day walking the length of river you intend to visit and get to know all its peculiarities, depths, possible snags and so on. It's a different world after dark and you can easily be caught out.

The Towy is true sea-trouting experience and one that is widely available for the visiting angler. You might have caught many a rainbow trout from a reservoir or stocked pond in the past, but to call yourself a true fly fisherman, you need to tangle with a Welsh sea trout at some time or another in your life!

☀ SEASON – 2 April to 7 October.

✦ TICKETS – day and weekly permits are available from a wide variety of sources. Try the Carmarthen Amateur Anglers' Association. Weekly permits vary between £45 and £55. The Carmarthen and District Angling Association offers day tickets at £20. Phone Tight Lines, 72 Wind Street, Ammanford on 01269 595858. The Cross Hands and District Angling Association has several blocks of fishing on the Towy, contact Tight Lines for information.

→ DIRECTIONS – The A40 from Llandovery, through Llandeilo to Carmarthen follows the course of the River Towy, which can be reached from the northwest via Builth Wells along the A483, from Abergavenny via the A40, or from Swansea via the M4 and A48.

⊨ ACCOMMODATION – Capel Dewi Uchaf Country House, on 01267 290799 or e-mail uchaffarm@aol.com, is highly recommended and has a riverside setting. Try Golden Grove Arms, Llanarthhne on 01558 668551 – just yards from some of the best sea trout fishing in Wales. Or, contact Llanerchindda Farm, Llandovery, Carmarthenshire SA20 0NB on 01550 750274 or e-mail nick@cambrianway.com; a lovely setting, very good accommodation and local ghillies available. Edwinsford Fishery and Cottages offer over four miles of double-bank fishing on the Cothi; contact Jonathan Heron, Edwinsford Farmhouse, Talley, Llandeilo, SA19 7BX on 01558 685848 (telephone), 01558 685849 (fax), email: herons@edwinsfordestate.co.uk (www.edwinsfordestate.co.uk).

GLYNCORRWG PONDS – GLAMORGAN

This is yet another Welsh jewel, hidden in a small isolated valley of the River Corrwg, a tributary of the Afan, and set amidst the nine-thousand-acre Afan Forest Park. The development of Glyncorrwg began over a decade ago, when the Countryside Commission donated half a million pounds to create the three pools. The trout fishing lake is a gem, not large at a couple of acres, but with depths reaching fifteen feet – sufficient to keep the fish cool in the summer and to give shelter in the winter. The lake is stream-fed and generally crystal clear, which allows good sight fishing.

There are both browns and rainbows in the water. The browns average perhaps little more than a pound and a half, but there are always stocks of fish to five pounds or more. The rainbows go in at around two pounds but grow on well and have been caught well into double figures.

In warmish weather, the fish are always willing to take from the surface but it's also an idea to take along a slow-sinking line and some heavier nymphs if you want to get amongst those big browns that keep low down in the water. Don't be in too much of a hurry to move either: it's interesting that a brown will often take a fly after it's been drawn over its head a number of times. In short, this is an interesting water in a stunning location.

⚘ SEASON – open all year.

⚡ TICKETS – phone the manager on 01639 851900 for bookings. Costs are £30 for a six-fish limit, £20 for a four-fish limit, £15 for a three-fish limit and £10 for a two-fish limit.

➜ DIRECTIONS – leave the M4 on junction 40 and take the A4107 to Cwmafan. When you reach the village of Cymer, take the turning left for Glyncorrwg. The fishery is about one mile along on your left.

⊨ ACCOMMODATION – Wales Tourist Board can provide information about various kinds of accommodation. Contact them on 029 2049 9909 or write to Brunel House, 2 Fitzalan Road, Cardiff CF24 0UY.

RAVENSNEST – GWENT

Ravensnest nestles in the beautiful Wye valley, with Tintern Abbey only a mile away, so you couldn't have a better setting for a fishery. Indeed, it's hard to believe that it's only ten minutes or so from the M4 and the old Severn Bridge. Another beauty of Ravensnest is that it's more like fishing a river than a still water. The two pools that make up the fishery are fed by the Angid stream and so have a constant flow. Perhaps favourite conditions are during the dry spell, when both pools become gin-clear and stalking the very big fish that the waters hold is a distinct possibility. Mind you, when there is a tinge of colour in the water, the fishing is frequently easier.

This is truly a great stalking water with plenty of high banks to give you good views of what is going on. The fish themselves are also of excellent quality and fight magnificently, especially when the water is crystal. Recommended flies are buzzers, black ones in particular, mayflies, damsels, but also take a selection of nymphs.

There is plenty of variety amongst the fish as well. You'd expect the rainbows and possibly the browns, but not the blues and the goldies, which can look truly spectacular. All in all, this is a beautifully-run, friendly fishery that sets some fascinating challenges in very beautiful countryside.

⚘ SEASON – Ravensnest is open all year.

⚡ TICKETS – contact the owner Simon Bridge on 01291 689564 or write to him at

Ravensnest, Raglan Road, Tintern, Chepstow, Gwent. Costs are £8 for a six-fish limit, or £3.50 per fish, up to a six-fish limit.

🎣 RECORDS – the biggest rainbow weighed in at 26lb 3oz.

🕴 FACILITIES – the lodge at Ravensnest is purpose built, with its own toilets. Food and soft drinks are available along with flies and some tackle. Tuition can also be arranged.

➜ DIRECTIONS – take junction 4 off the M48 and head for Chepstow. At the first roundabout, carry straight on, passing the racecourse. At St Arvans, turn left, signposted Devauden. Carry on until you see a sign for The Cott. Turn left here onto the Tintern road. The fishery is one mile further down on your right.

🛏 ACCOMMODATION – there is plenty of guesthouse and bed and breakfast accommodation in Chepstow and up the road towards Tintern. Wales Tourist Board, Brunel House, 2 Fitzalan Road, Cardiff CR24 0UY will be able to advise. Contact them on 029 2049 9909.

THE RIVER USK – POWYS

The River Usk becomes everyone's favourite river once they've fished it. It rises in the Brecon Beacons and then runs in that wonderful, unspoilt countryside between the Beacons themselves and the Black Mountains, before disgorging out into the Bristol Channel at Newport. Until a few years ago, the Usk seemed to be in trouble, but a renaissance is thankfully taking place. A plan by Newport Borough Council to build a barrage across the estuary has, fortunately, been scotched, and a lot of work is being done by the Environment Agency and the United Usk Fishermen's Association to encourage salmon to return and also to improve the river habitat for all species. If proof is needed that the Usk is once again a flourishing, fertile river, all you need to do is look at the number of dippers, the contented state of the herons and the return of the otters.

Above all, the Usk is, and always has been, famous for its stocks of wild brown trout – fish averaging around ten to twelve ounces, but frequently topping the pound. And what fish they are! I remember, with absolute joy, taking six wild browns from a half-mile length of broken white water one afternoon in 1997, and each one made me draw breath as I looked at it. A little bit of paradise indeed. In the early season, late March and April, try march browns tied on a ten or twelve, olive nymphs on a twelve or a fourteen or small hare's ears. As the summer begins to warm up, evening and blue duns and light olives take over. In the high summer, it's difficult to beat light and dark Sedges, Ginger quills, copper Tups, Badgers and the whole gamut of nymphs.

To get the best out of Usk, you will need to wade the river. Travel gently, though, taking care not to scrunch on the stones as these wildies really are poised for flight. Be careful of your shadow, and beware of a line falling loosely, as the slightest mistake will result in arrows of fleeing, panicked trout.

Salmon are holding their own on the Usk and nowhere will you find better water than that offered by the Gliffaes Country House Hotel near Crichowell. There are perfect holding pools and there's evidence that the large springers for which the river was once renowned could be poised for a return.

☀ **SEASON** – the trout opens on 3 March and closes on 30 September. Salmon fishing also begins on 3 March but ends on 17 October. For salmon, it is fly fishing only until 16 June and all fish must be returned. After 16 June, spinning is permitted and caught salmon may be kept. The hotel wisely encourages its fishermen to return salmon later in the season nearer spawning time. Big females should always be returned.

🐟 **TICKETS** – tickets at Gliffaes cost £25 per day for salmon and £20 per day for trout; the brown trout fishing is top quality. Hotel residents take priority but all fishermen are welcomed. It makes sense, obviously, to phone the hotel to check on availability before travelling. Call free on 0800 146719. The water is split into beats with rods restricted to two on each length.

➜ **DIRECTIONS** – Crichowell lies northeast of Abergavenny on the A40 Brecon road. Two and a half miles west of Crichowell, Gliffaes is signposted to the left. Follow this road for a mile and you will arrive at the gates of the hotel.

🛏 **ACCOMMODATION** – I've always fished the Usk at Gliffaes and I don't think you could find a better base. At least, you'd be doing yourself a favour to start there, especially as the information you will receive on the two and a half miles of water is absolutely first rate.

🎓 **TUITION** – the hotel offers periodic courses on everything to do with wild river fishing. Phone the hotel for details.

❧ HIGHLY RECOMMENDED FISHERIES ❧

- *Hayricks Lake, Nr. Merthyr Tydfil, Glamorgan. Phone 01443 829262 for details. Well stocked and attractive. Catch and release also.*
- *Gludy Lake, Brecon, Powys. Call 01874 610427 for more information. Truly beautiful water. Great fish. Very secluded. Marvellous lodge and log cabin accommodation. Highly recommended.*
- *Llandegfedd, Pontypool. Contact on 01291 673722. Four hundred and thirty acres. Well stocked. Good fleet of boats. Lovely situation.*
- *Pantyreos, Newport, Gwent. Fourteen-acre reservoir in lovely surroundings. Catch and release. Fighting fit fish.*
- *Plasynant Fishery, Anglesey. Some excellent fish in a nice situation.*
- *Valley Dam Fishery, Denbighshire. Phone for details on 01691 648837. Super quality fish. Good surface fishing.*
- *Llyn Gwyn, Nr. Builth Wells, Powys. Phone 01597 811099. Stunning location with awe-inspiring views. Good stocking levels, Some big fish.*
- *Peterstone Trout Lake, Newport, Gwent. Phone 01633 680905. Generous stocking with good-sized fish, average three pounds and plenty of doubles. Lures work well, but try buzzers as the water warms.*

FLY-FISHING SITES IN THE NORTH

1. Pennine Fishery
2. Loveclough
3. Raygill Fishery
4. The River Wharfe
5. The River Nidd
6. Lockwood Beck
7. Gyllhead Trout Fishery
8. Esthwaite Water
9. Dubbs Trout Fishery
10. High Newton Trout Fish
11. The River Eden
12. The River Till
13. Coldingham Loch

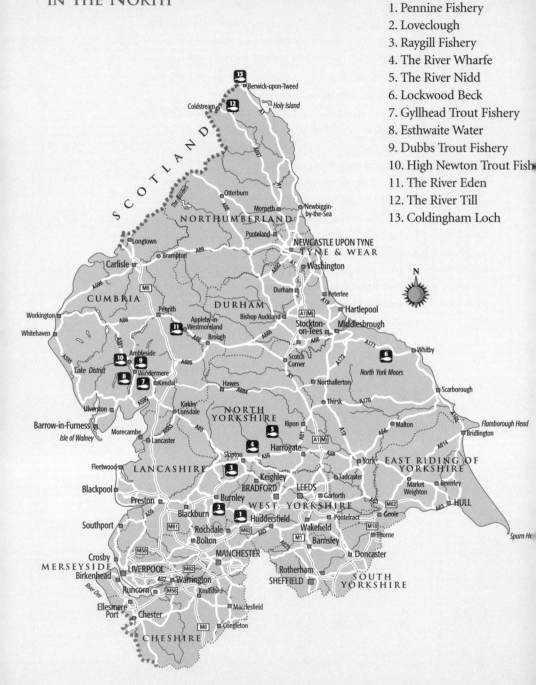

'*I've fished the Lakes now for forty years, since I was a boy of seven, and reckon I know a fair bit about them. For me, fly fishing in the Lake District has always been about adventures, long walks, steep climbs to find untouched fish and crystal clear streams, gin-like lakes or tumbling spate rivers. There's so much mystery around – perhaps my favourite place is Wast Water, the deepest and clearest lake in England, overshadowed by Scafell, the country's highest mountain. I also love the variety of fish in the Lake District – superb salmon fishing if you know where to find it, and the sea trout can be an absolute dream. The trout of the tarns are also special, often silver with jet-black spots. If you know where to catch them, you can find char as well – those fabulous, flitting little bird-like fish from the Ice Age.*'

ALISTAIR NICHOLSON – FISHING TV PRESENTER AND WRITER

So that's on the west of the area – how about the east? Karen Brunton of the Northumberland Rivers' Project has this to say: 'Northumberland is often ignored in the game fishers' lemming-like annual stampede to cross the Scottish border, but its clean rivers, fresh lakes and vast reservoirs are a priceless jewel set in a varied and dramatic landscape. The main waters of the north and south Tyne, Till, Coquet, Aln and Wansbeck host an increasing abundance of salmon and trout on beats that remain accessible and affordable. Some great fishing in some magnificent countryside'.

How do you even begin to describe the wealth of fly fishing that is available in that broad band from Cumbria, through Lancashire and Yorkshire up to Durham and Northumberland? There's just about everything available, from tiny browns to huge rainbows – there is even a good number of salmon about. And you've got the char of Windermere to boot! This area encompasses some of our most rugged, unspoilt countryside.

PENNINE FISHERY – LANCASHIRE

Pennine Fishery has built up a really grand reputation in the north-west
for many very good reasons. The fish stocked are invariably in really good
condition and, moreover, they're big. It's not unusual to see double-figure
fish cruising around, and even twenties are in the water. Also, Pennine is a
challenging sort of place. Perched up in the moors, the weather is
frequently unpredictable and there's often a good chop on the water but
that doesn't mean you can get away with heavy gear or stereotyped fishing.
No, far from it, Pennine really does demand that you think about what
you're doing, assess the ever-changing situation and fish intelligently.

There are two lakes at Pennine, both well stocked and deep. Try buzzers,
on the surface and also down deeper. Dry flies can work, especially in the
evening when big fish will come up to the surface. Lures are worth a spin,
especially if you see a big fish feeding in close. What you are unlikely to get
at Pennine are grab-and-smash-type takes. The fish are wary and it's often a
good idea to have a sight indicator on your leader if you're fishing small
nymphs or buzzers down deep. You often just won't pick up takes otherwise.

Pennine is a beautiful, peaceful place to fish and there's a very friendly
atmosphere about the place. It's built up a tremendous reputation, so it's a
good idea to book a ticket before making the journey.

☀ **SEASON** – Pennine is open all year round.

✹ **TICKETS** – contact Lee Moran at Pennine Fishery, Caldebrook Road, Littleborough, Nr.
Rochdale, Lancs on 01706 378325. An eight-hour, three-fish ticket costs £24.85. A four-hour,
two-fish ticket is £16.90. An eight-hour sporting ticket costs £16, for four hours it's £12.50.

⚖ **RECORDS** – at present the rainbow record is 29lb 7oz, the brown trout record 24lb 11oz
and golden trout 14lb 8oz.

➡ **DIRECTIONS** – from Rochdale, take the A58 to Littleborough. Before reaching the town
centre, take the White Lees road and continue until it becomes Caldebrook Road. The fishery
is a mile further on and very easily seen.

⊨ **ACCOMMODATION** – contact the Tourist Information Centre in Rochdale on 01706 356592
for details of various kinds of accommodation in the area.

LOVECLOUGH – LANCASHIRE

Loveclough is a dramatic water indeed, perched high amidst the moorland
of the Rossendale valley. The water is only about three acres but somehow
its spacious surroundings give it a more ample, totally uncramped feel –
it's probably got something to do with the fabulous views over the curlew-
haunted countryside. But let's get to the fishing, which can be stunning.
Although the water is quite deep, dropping to twenty-three feet from a

ledge at fourteen feet, most anglers still like to fish on or near the surface. Indeed, Loveclough is very much a dry fly man's paradise and you can pick fish up on buzzers even in the winter. There might be times in the heat of the summer months when a sinking line can get you down to skulking fish, but even then most of the regulars would rather use a long leader and a heavy nymph to search deeper water.

The water is generally very clear indeed, and only occasionally colours up a little after very heavy rain, which clouds the feeder stream. For the rest, the springs tend to maintain a remarkable clarity, which helps fish spotting. There's generally a breeze at this sort of altitude and Loveclough is open to the elements. However, a slight chop is perfect for the dry-fly man. In a brisk wind, stay clear of a three fly team and fish one or, at the most, two flies until you're really practised in the art. In fact, my own preference has always been for just the one. Cast across the wind and let your fly drift naturally, covering as much water as you possibly can; you'll find that very frequently this method picks out the canniest of the fish. Remember that a fish that has seen a lot before will often want to study a fly before making up its mind.

Loveclough is stocked with fish in the one-and-a-half- to two-pound bracket, and what glorious specimens they are, both rainbows and browns.

❊ FLUOROCARBON ❊

Fluorocarbon leaders are now all the rage. But what is fluorocarbon? Basically, it's a chemical fusion of fluoride and carbon, which makes for a stiff and abrasion-resistant material.

- *A major advantage of fluorocarbon is that it has a refractive index so close to that of water that it is nearly invisible under the surface. In clear venues, this can be a huge step forward.*
- *A further advantage is that fluorocarbons sink very quickly. This is very useful when trying to get small flies like buzzers and nymphs down to the depths. Ordinary monofilament is much more slow sinking.*
- *Be careful with fluorocarbons if you're using dry flies. They can sink under the weight.*
- *Take care with your knots. An ordinary half-blood knot will work, but you must tie it carefully. Don't attempt to attach fluorocarbon to nylon.*
- *There are now many different fluorocarbons on the market. Take your time and try to trial test as many as possible. Once you've settled on the one for you, stick with it and build up your confidence.*

The management team requests that you return the latter. There are also big numbers of fish in the eight- to eleven-pound bracket, with rainbows of fourteen to fifteen pounds caught and seen. Now imagine one of those sipping in your Black Gnat as dusk begins to creep across the moorland!

⚓ **SEASON** – Loveclough is open all year apart from Christmas Day and New Year's Day.

🎣 **TICKETS** – contact Mrs G. Dumbill, Loveclough Fishery, Commercial Street, Loveclough, Rossendale, Lancashire on 01706 212541. A four-fish, full-day ticket costs £20, a two-fish, half-day (six hours) ticket costs £14 and a one-fish, three-hour ticket is £7.50. Catch and release is also available at £2 per hour.

➜ **DIRECTIONS** – the village of Loveclough is situated on the A682 between Rawtenstall and Burnley. If you're travelling northwards, Commercial Street is on the left-hand side of the main road and the fishery is clearly signposted.

🛏 **ACCOMMODATION** – information about a variety of accommodation can be obtained from the Tourist Information Centre in Accrington on 01254 872595.

RAYGILL FISHERY – YORKSHIRE

Raygill is an extraordinary place, as far as the trout fisherman is concerned. It is made up of two lakes – one comparatively small at just over an acre and the second one at eight and a half acres. This is sunk deep into a disused limestone quarry with vertical cliffs around its perimeter – a truly dramatic setting for a very peaceful and very intelligently-run fishery.

Realising that the days of the big bag merchants are pretty much now on the wane, a sporting ticket has been introduced at Raygill, which is all the rage. Most fish are returned and this has increased the size of the fish and the challenge of the water.

Everything about Raygill is on a big scale – the deep water so close in shore, the clarity, and the shadows of the huge fish you can see crisscrossing beneath you. It's an exciting place to fish without any doubt. Mind you, even despite the depths, the fish are very easy to tempt to the surface and some of the biggest of the boys fall to well-fished buzzers. But remember that many of the fish have been caught and released and everything has to be fished intelligently if it's going to be successful. Once again, there's no magic fly – it's a matter of how it's fished.

Of course, you can put on a fast-sinking line and really try to plumb the depths. On hot days especially, this approach can reap its rewards, but you don't always have to go deep at Raygill. Daddies, for example, work very well later on in the summer and in the early autumn. There are also a good number of roach and bream fry appearing, and any fly patterns take their share of fish, so don't forget your Zonkers and Muddlers.

The management has also set about another experiment. A good number of big pike have been introduced on the smaller trout lake. It's an interesting idea, the concept being that these big fish – all of them big doubles – actually profit from any dying or failing rainbows. The idea seems to have been a success so far – the pike have grown on quickly and the quality of the rainbows has increased substantially. Pike fishing now is very popular amongst some of the locals and only recently a pike of thirty pounds and four ounces was taken on a six-inch fry pattern fly! Quite an achievement.

SEASON – open all year. Fishing is from 8.30am to dusk.

TICKETS – write to the Fishery Manager, Raygill Fishery, 1 Raygill Cottage, Lothersdale, Skipton, North Yorkshire or contact him on 01535 632500. Sporting tickets cost £2 per hour or £12 for the full day. All fish are returned. Any fish can be taken at a cost of £1.75 per pound. Big fish are increasingly popular for a Christmas treat.

RECORDS – the fish grow on very quickly at Raygill and the rainbow record is 21lb 8oz with many double figure fish. The browns are stocked at about ten inches or so but they grow quickly to 5lb plus.

DIRECTIONS – from the end of the M65 eastbound, take the A6068 and then turn left for Lothersdale. Go down the steep hill to the village. At the bottom, take the turning for the caravan site. The fishery is then four hundred yards along on the left. From Skipton, take the A629 and turn right on the outskirts of the town onto the Carleton Road, signposted Carleton and Lothersdale. Once you enter Lothersdale, keep the pub on the right and drive through the village. At the bend in the road, take the left turning for the caravan site.

ACCOMMODATION – the Tourist Information Centre in Skipton on 01756 792809 will be able to supply information on various kinds of accommodation available.

THE RIVER WHARFE – YORKSHIRE

Of all the Dales rivers, the Wharfe is perhaps the most beloved and the most typical of this alternately rugged and lush Yorkshire countryside. The Wharfe itself rises on Cam Fell and flows sixty miles south-east to join the Ouse. There are coarse fish in its lower reaches but it's the trout fishing higher up that is really exceptional.

Probably the easiest and certainly the most dramatic opportunities for the visiting angler exist at Bolton Abbey, the famous estate of the Duke of Devonshire. The River Wharfe flows through the centre of the estate and offers spectacular fishing. It flows over limestone and the excellent quality of the water is reflected in the abundance of fly life and the exceptional condition of the brown trout. Bolton Abbey is a wondrous place to fish. Dippers, sandpipers, kingfishers, sand martins, warblers, swifts and swallows all make fishing there in the summer an unforgettable experience.

The fishing isn't always easy – the frequently low, crystal-clear water sees to that. Also, it has to be said that Bolton Abbey is visited by many non-anglers and the trout do get wary of the shadows cast. However, the river bailiff – certainly the one I met – proved to be exceptionally helpful. As a good standard, he recommended the Grey Duster as the outstanding dry fly pretty well season round. Going sub-surface, he suggested that the pheasant-tailed nymph was hard to beat. Mind you, he also had a leaning towards the partridge in orange, partridge in yellow and the treacle Parkin.

There are beats of this river that you just cannot afford to miss. Fish around at the Strid early in the morning before the sightseers arrive. There is something primeval about the spectacular point where the Wharfe surges through its narrow gorge. Best of all, though, move down to the Priory around sunset and pick up a fish or two as the shafts of light trace their shadows on the ancient brickwork. Yes, Bolton Abbey is an exhilarating place to catch a trout or a grayling.

❧ A Handful of Tips ❧

It's often a good idea to keep on the move if you're bank fishing, rather than stay in one spot, to avoid the trout getting spooked.

- *A change of fly is always a good idea after you've fished in the same place for a while. If you've been fishing white, try black. If you've been fishing big, try small. Anything that is different can trigger a response.*
- *If you see fish swirling on the surface but you're not getting any takes to a dry fly, it could be that the fish are taking insects just beneath the surface, emerging before hatching. In this case, try a team of buzzers fished just a few inches beneath the surface.*
- *Try fishing into the wind. Casting is more difficult, but fish will be concentrated in the downwind areas and the chances are most anglers will have tended to avoid them.*
- *Only put on a finer leader if you're absolutely sure that's the only way to get a take. There's not much point hooking that fish only to lose it.*
- *Don't panic. The temptation is to try to cast further and further and probably get into more tangles. Instead, take a rest, sit down and think things out. If somebody else is catching, then take time to watch and, if need be, ask a couple of polite questions.*
- *Remember that learning is all-important. It's not as though you need to catch those fish to live, so enjoyment should be the name of the game.*

⛅ **SEASON** – trout fishing runs from the 1 April to 30 September. Trout and grayling combined run from 16 June to 30 September. Grayling tickets only are available from 1 October to 22 December.

🎣 **TICKETS** – these are available for fishing the estate waters – around four and a half miles along both banks – from the Estate Office, Monday to Friday from 9.00am to 10.00am and 9.30am to 10.30am on Saturday and Sunday. Phone 01756 710227 for further details. The adult day ticket is £20 and the junior day ticket is £5.

🐟 **RULES** – fishing is permitted between 9.00am to one hour after sunset. A beat will be allocated to you, which you must adhere to until 3.00pm after which you can fish any stretch of the river beneath the aqueduct as far as Kex Beck. The fishery is very tightly managed for the good of these excellently-conditioned trout. You can only use a barbless hook – a £75 fine for transgressors! No hooks must be used larger than a size twelve, which rules out lures and reservoir flies. Also, all returns must be completed even if no fish have been taken.

➔ **DIRECTIONS** – As you head east from Skipton towards Harrogate along the A59, turn left onto the B6160 and Bolton Abbey is less than a mile north.

🛏 **ACCOMMODATION** – there is a wealth of bed and breakfast accommodation in the area. Particularly recommended is Bondcroft Farm on 01756 793571. Alternatives include Heskith Farm Cottage on 01756 710541 (just three quarters of a mile from the Priory itself), The Manor House on 01756 730226, Langerton Farm on 01756 730260 and Holmhouse Farm on 01756 720661. The Devonshire Arms Country House Hotel is right on the river itself and offers superb food and accommodation. Highly recommended. Phone 01756 710441.

THE RIVER NIDD – YORKSHIRE

The Nidd is a lovely Yorkshire river that holds coarse fish lower down its reaches but offers spectacular trout and grayling fishing nearer to its source. Perhaps the easiest access to wonderful water for the visitor is offered by Nidderdale Angling Club who control about eleven miles of the mid river. And what wonderful water it is – full of charm and character, often overhung by trees as it winds through lush meadowland. Deep pools, twists and turns, dancing shallows – everything is here.

I enjoyed an enchanting May day just beneath Pately Bridge a couple of years back. My companion and I did not see another angler even though it was Sunday and the weather was fine. But we did see fish. Five grayling of around a pound and as many trout – including a stunner of a pound and a half – made the day. Most were caught on nymphs, as you might expect early in the season, but two fish fell to a Grey Duster and the biggest grayling rose to sip in a Green Wells.

The day was also made complete for me by watching a number of brook lampreys digging their nests ready for spawning. In one place, the gravels were alive with these tiny eel-like creatures just four or five inches long.

When I have fished and found other anglers, I've been overwhelmed with the warm welcome and generous advice: that's the way of things up in Yorkshire. The term 'the brotherhood of the angle' still holds fast here and if you've got a question you know it will be answered directly.

✦ TICKETS – Nidderdale Angling Club issue day tickets for £8 per person at the Post Offices in the villages of Lofthouse, Pateley Bridge, Glasshouses and Summerbridge. Anglers must obtain tickets before fishing.

🗨 RULES – although the club owns most of the water on both banks, do consult maps and make sure that you do not trespass on the occasional private beats. Take great care with gates as there are frequently livestock grazing the riverbanks. For the same reasons, take even greater care with any discarded nylon, bags or other rubbish.

➔ DIRECTIONS – Pateley Bridge lies between Ripon and Skipton on the B6265.

🛏 ACCOMMODATION – the Tourist Information Centre in Ripon on 01765 604625 will be able to supply information about various kinds of accommodation available in the area.

LOCKWOOD BECK – YORKSHIRE

I really enjoyed my day on Lockwood Beck a couple of years ago for several reasons. Firstly, the sixty-four-acre water is stunningly beautiful, set high on the moors with panoramic views all round. Secondly, I enjoyed the warmth of the welcome and the advice freely passed on to me by the regulars. And then, inevitably, there was the fishing. Lockwood browns and rainbows are big, beautifully finned and fight magnificently... as well as setting a really serious challenge.

Lockwood is an old reservoir, Victorian I think, but that doesn't really matter. What is important is that it is now leased from Northumbria Water and, because it is no longer used for water supply, the levels remain constant. It's got a really spacious feel to it and, because the boats are propelled by oars or your own electric engine, there's a real serenity. The management here is truly far thinking. Firstly, the quality of the fish is outstanding. You really won't find nicer rainbows anywhere. Secondly, you've got the added bonus that the water produces its own natural wild brown stock and these fish are quite spectacular, sometimes running to seven or eight pounds or even more. The rumour is that there's even the odd double in there. The reason? Well, there are lots of perch fry, huge stocks of minnows and stone loach and Lockwood anyway is very rich in insect life. All in all, a perfect combination.

Fishing is pretty well year round. You can catch fish on buzzers even in winter and, when the weather's mild, on dry fly. Daphnia can be a slight problem in the summer – good for fish growth obviously but the very devil if you're trying to entice a fish to take a small nymph.

A perfect wild brown trout from a northern Yorkshire stream. Although this fish was little over a pound, the strength of its fight was astonishing, and that big, shovel-like tail fin explains why.

The valleys of the north are dotted with little streams that often escape the fly fisher's notice. A polite request will often result in permission being granted. Watch out for small but beautiful wild browns.

As the environment changes, salmon runs are beginning to fluctuate also. Once, rivers would have early runs or late ones, but now the boundaries are becoming blurred, so check the best time to fish.

Scotland is the home of char – delicate, beautiful fish – and they should be returned at once. These were actually caught in Greenland, where eating them was a necessary act of survival.

Fishing the spate rivers of the north and the west is an exciting sport. Wading is almost always essential, but take care. A wading stick helps, and make sure your boots are felted and studded.

A magnificent, fresh run, Atlantic salmon. Although the species has struggled in recent years there's every chance that a revival is taking place. The trend towards catch and release can only help this.

You'll get lots of advice when you arrive at Lockwood, and everybody has their own solution. Catches do seem to be divided reasonably equally between bank and boat fishermen but I personally enjoy fishing the boat. The big key, as always, is not to over extend yourself for a fish thirty yards away, but simply sit tight and fish neat and close so you don't disturb those that are within easy casting range. Let yourself drift and you'll soon come close to feeding fish. At times, you look round at Lockwood and see fish everywhere. Mind you, it might look easy but it very rarely is! So, look for top of the water sport with small flies in the summer but don't forget muddlers, Cats Whiskers and so on if you're looking for the odd big wild brown. But they can, and do, come on virtually anything. I'm told that Christmas time is particularly good, though quite why that should be nobody seems to know.

❧ EXTENDING THE USE OF BUZZERS ❧

Buzzers are increasingly an integral part of the fly-fishing scene, especially on still waters. Traditionally, buzzers have been fished either in the surface film or just inches beneath it, but it is possible to fish buzzers on quick-sink lines – very effective, especially in winter. Trout can, and will, take buzzers on the drop as they sink, during the retrieve, on the lift or as you hang the flies in front of the boat.

- *Firstly, let your flies drop for as long as possible before pulling them back. Use slender flies dressed on heavyweight hooks.*
- *Keep in touch with your flies as they are sinking through the water – it's important if you're going to feel that take.*
- *Try different retrieve rates as you're bringing the flies back to the boat or the bank. It's a good idea sometimes to let them simply hang static for a moment to try and trick a trout that's been following.*
- *Remember takes can be very gentle. Always look where the line enters the water and strike if you see a slight tightening. Occasionally, also, your rod tip might just twitch.*
- *Don't get disillusioned if you don't pick up fish instantly. Deep water buzzer work can sometimes be slow but then is enlivened by frenetic activity. This is triggered by a deep water buzzer hatch.*
- *Try to animate your flies as much as possible, vary the retrieve and always, always concentrate so you can pick up that very delicate take.*

⚓ SEASON – there is generally a two-week closed season about the beginning of March whilst the water is rested and restocked. All stocked fish are over two pounds in weight.

🎣 TICKETS – contact Lockwood Fishery, Nr. Guisborough, North Yorkshire on 01287 660501. There are several ticket structures but basically £20 will buy you a four-fish ticket, with catch and release included. An evening ticket costs £15, and for this you can take two fish and release others. A ticket for any four hours is £10, and for this you can catch one and release others. Boats cost £12 for a day including permit, or £8 in the evening. Outboard hire is £5. From November or thereabouts, a different price structure kicks in with cheaper fishing as stocking ceases, but there are always plenty of fish in the water. In the summer, fishing begins at 8.00am, and at the end of October at 10.00am.

🎣 RECORDS – rainbows of around 15lb have been recorded, and browns over 12lb.

➡ DIRECTIONS – from Guisborough, just south-west of Middlesbrough, take the A171 towards Whitby. After about five miles, you will see the reservoir on the right – it is well signposted.

🛏 ACCOMMODATION – there is a variety of accommodation available in nearby Whitby and Scarborough. Contact the Tourist Information Offices in these two towns on 01947 602674 (Whitby) and 01723 3733333 (Scarborough) for further details. There is also good bed and breakfast accommodation in the small villages on the North Yorkshire moors.

GYLLHEAD TROUT FISHERY – CUMBRIA

Gyllhead is a beautifully matured reservoir in the hills to the south-east of Lake Windermere, with fabulous views of the south lakeland mountains, especially on summer evenings. The reservoir is long and thin, winding along a steep valley for most of its eleven acres. Virtually all the shoreline is fishable and several small streams feed the reservoir, the fresh water often attracting fish in close. The deepest water is down by the dam, at around seventeen feet, and it gradually tapers towards the shallows of three feet or less at the far end. At least two thirds of the reservoir is, however, ten feet or more in depth. There are a few browns that are naturally sustaining, so if you do catch one of these the WADAA, who control the water expertly, plead with you to return them. You will mostly catch rainbows, and the average size of stock is around a pound and a half, though there are a number of bigger fish, several in excess of five or six pounds.

There are plenty of fish-holding features, but it makes sense on a water like this to keep on the move. Fish one area intently and then move on until fish are contacted. Most of the regulars tend to fish a floating line, with a long or short leader depending on where they're expecting to find fish. In the cold weather, fish will certainly be found in the deeper water, but during the summer they move into the bays and shallows where you'll often find them feeding on buzzers and dry flies. In very hot weather, they will once again be in the deeps, often close to the springs that offer cool, oxygenated water. It's at times like this that a very fast-sinking line can work wonders, especially if you're using a fly that has to be worked quickly.

As for flies, try Vivas and Black Chenille very early in the season, but don't forget buzzer hatches will be occurring by late March and certainly into April. By May, lake olives will be seen, and as the summer progresses trout will begin to fry feed and chase daddy longlegs. But, once again, remember that buzzers work pretty well throughout the entire season. And anyway, it's not the fly, as they say, it's the driver.

Gyllhead, with its steep banks, is well sheltered from the winds that frequently pound the Lakes, so it's a good water to go to if conditions are stormy. In fact, come to that, it's a good water to visit anytime, simply to bask in the peace and serenity.

Season – starts on 15 March and finishes on 31 December.

Tickets – Gyllhead Reservoir is controlled by the Windermere, Ambleside and District Angling Association. Tickets are available from Carlsons Fishing Tackle, call 01539 724867 or visit www.carlsons.co.uk. A two-fish day ticket costs £12 and catch and release is then allowed, providing it is carried out sensitively.

Directions – take the A592 from Windermere towards Bowness. Turn first right into the small lane signposted Cartmel Fell Road. The trout fishery is on the right-hand side of the road after half a mile. Car parking is available on the left, half way along the reservoir.

Accommodation – phone the Tourist Information Centre in Windermere on 015394 46499 or in Ambleside on 015394 32582 for details of the plentiful accommodation.

Esthwaite Water – Cumbria

Esthwaite is one of Cumbria's most beautiful waters, situated just to the west of Windermere in the most magnificent rolling, tree-rich countryside. It's a large lake – nearly three hundred acres – split into two basins. The north basin is fly only, whereas any method goes in the south. It's a very prolific water, with huge hatches of buzzer and caddis fly. Damsel fly and corixa also feature large. The trout average something between a pound and a pound and a half, but on their rich diet, they soon grow on to become beautiful, silvery fish – often large in size. The fishery record is twelve pounds, and there are probably rainbows lurking that could smash that. And, to add a bit of spice, there are also some large wild brown trout. Again, the record is nine pounds and eight ounces, but who knows?

You don't have to take a boat out on Esthwaite but it probably helps if you want to explore everything the water has to offer. In the same way, it's wise to hedge your bets when it comes to the fishing.

On cold, windy days or hot, still ones, you might well find the fish down deep and that a sinking line is necessary. But, for the most part, a floating line will probably do, along with a team of buzzers. Remember, as I've already said, this is a very buzzer-rich water indeed. A final tip – don't work your buzzers too quickly at all on Esthwaite. Indeed, in a mild breeze, simply let them drift, giving them the odd tweak now and again.

☀ SEASON – open all year.

⚡ TICKETS – contact David Coleman at Esthwaite Water Trout Fishery, The Boathouse, Hawkshead, Cumbria on 01539 436541. Day ticket prices are £21, with a four-fish limit. Evening tickets (4pm – sunset) are £13, with a two-fish limit. A boat for two costs £58 per day, with reduced boat charges from November to February inclusive. The boats are powered by electric engines.

👤 FACILITIES – lodge with tackle shop, toilets and plenty of coffee!

🛡 RECORDS – rainbow trout 16lb 4oz, brown trout 9lb 8oz.

➔ DIRECTIONS – from the M6 leave at junction 36 and follow the A590 to the Newby Bridge roundabout. Stay on the A590 towards Barrow. Turn right at the signpost for Lakeside and Hawkshead, passing through Lakeside. Continue for about seven miles and the fishery is well-signposted on the right.

⊨ ACCOMMODATION – the Tourist Information Centre in Windermere can provide details of a variety of accommodation in the area. Phone for details on 015394 46499.

DUBBS TROUT FISHERY – CUMBRIA

Dubbs is one of my absolute favourite still-water trout fisheries in the north. It's way up in the hills, seven hundred and fifty feet above sea level, with superb views. It is well off the beaten track and can be difficult to find – it's a good job that day permits have a detailed location map on the rear!

Dubbs is not a water for the fainthearted. It's gin-clear and, being very highly alkaline, has a rich and varied aquatic life. This means that there's a great deal of natural food and the trout, which are stocked on a fortnightly basis, don't always respond to the fly easily. They will come to the surface if there is a plentiful hatch but often you won't see them because they've got food enough down deep. Mind you, when they are on the top, Dubbs' trout are really scintillating. You can sometimes get a buzzer hatch or a summer evening rise to caenis, and you'll find top water sport. Equally, spring and autumn olives and summer sedges can give rise to periods of frantic activity and small black flies can be relied upon to bring fish up on any overcast day.

Still, you've got to consider nymphs if you're going to experience action throughout the day. Most of the bank sees you casting into water around ten feet deep, so this can be tackled on a floating line with leaders up to twenty or twenty-five feet. A slow sinking line can be used off the dam, however. You can get away with one or two quite heavily leaded nymphs as Dubbs does remain remarkably weed free throughout the summer and seldom presents problems to a deep-fished fly. The Pheasant Tail is always a good Dubbs' standby, as is a Hare's Ear. As for buzzers, on my limited visits I've found black and olive colours to be as good as anything. Locals tell you that the wind has a big effect on Dubbs – not surprising, as it's a relatively open water at altitude – and if the wind is from the east, just don't bother!

⛏ SEASON – starts on 15 March and finishes on 31 December.

🎣 TICKETS – Dubbs is controlled by the Windermere, Ambleside and District Angling Association. Permits are available from the Service Station at Ings on the A591 and also from the Tourist Information Centres in Windermere and Ambleside (see below).

🛡 RECORDS – the average size of fished stocked is a 1lb 8oz, but frequent fish of 8lb plus are introduced.

➡ DIRECTIONS – from the Ing Service Station on the A591, head towards Windermere and take the second turning on the right. Travel along this road for about a mile, ignoring the first small road on the right, to High Borrans. Dubbs road is about a quarter of a mile further, on the right, and is nothing more than a rough stone track. The fishery is about half a mile up the track. There is a car park near the dam.

🛏 ACCOMMODATION – the local Tourist Information Centres in Windermere on 015394 46499 and Ambleside on 015394 32582 will be able to recommend accommodation.

HIGH NEWTON TROUT FISHERY – CUMBRIA

High Newton is about eleven acres in extent, once again set in stunning scenery overlooking Morecambe Bay. It is stocked on a two weekly basis, with rainbows averaging nearly two pounds, along with some bigger fish approaching ten pounds. There's also an excellent population of wild brown trout, which go to a decent size. As is common with all WADAA waters, there is a two-fish limit, but catch and release, using barbless hooks is encouraged thereafter. The large tagged fish, by the way, must be released: they are put in to give added zest to what's already very good fishing.

Because of its altitude and lack of shelter, High Newton can be bleak early in the season when lures and weighted nymphs hold sway. Sport really begins in mid to late April when the daytime buzzer hatches begin. These peak in May and continue for much of the rest of the year, so always go prepared to fish Black or Suspender buzzers, especially into a slight ripple. Hawthorn fly are about from early May, and Beetles and other terrestrials keep the fish surface feeding right through the early summer. From mid June onwards, most surface activity is either early or late – especially in hot spells.

Then, buzzers and caenis can be prolific, with sedges hatching from mid July. Be careful of hot, still days in summer when the fish go dour and deep, but if you go on a mild, ripply sort of day, you'll get rises throughout. September and early October are cracking months at Newton and, providing the weather is reasonably kind, you'll see fish rising right into November.

Although High Newton is a stocked fishery, it's best to treat it as you would a moorland tarn and keep on the move. You'll sometimes find groups of fish but, as a general rule, the rainbows keep mobile and need tracking down. Equally, though lures do take their fair share, smaller imitative patterns are far more effective. Accurate casting is a must: target rising fish and you'll keep picking them up day long. Finally – don't the rainbows fight?

☀ **SEASON** – open from the 15 March to 31 December inclusive.

✸ **TICKETS** – these can be bought in advance from the Tourist Information Centres at Windermere on 015394 46499 and Ambleside on 015394 32582. They can also be purchased from Newby Bridge Motors at Newby Bridge on the A592.

➔ **DIRECTIONS** – to find the fishery, head towards High Newton on the A592 from Windermere. After a mile, you will pass a caravan site on the left-hand side of the road. The turn-off to High Newton is a small, concealed road about two hundred yards further, on the left. If you've passed the farm shop, then you've missed the turning. The reservoir is up the fell road, through two gates, which you must close. Parking is on the right, a hundred and fifty yards after the second gate.

⊨ **ACCOMMODATION** – details of a variety of accommodation can be obtained from the local Tourist Information Centre. Telephone numbers as above.

THE RIVERS EDEN AND TILL

Two of my most beloved northern rivers are frequently overlooked – the Eden in the west and the Till, a tributary of Tweed, in the east. I've classified them together as they're both the same sort of size, both hold salmon, sea trout, brown trout and grayling and, above all, both possess an intimate, and charming character. Rivers mean different things to different people, quite obviously, but a small river, for me anyway, speaks straight to the soul. Especially in surroundings as delightful as you'll find in these valleys.

Fishing on the Till is not always easily come by but when I've chanced upon it, I've had some quite glorious sport, with sea trout especially, the occasional salmon and magnificent grayling. It's one of the delights of the Tweed area that the 'lady of the stream' is so frequently overlooked. For grayling fishing on the Till, I favour a team of nymphs – two, or at the most three – fished close to the bottom under a tiny strike indicator. Takes are often minute, perhaps just a holding up of the line or a quick jab down.

Strike at once and you can easily find a fish of two pounds in weight on the end. Look for grayling in deep, pacy runs, perhaps where gravel or a sandbar dips down into deeper water. Keep everything tight and close and don't try to cast long distances. All that you'll do that way is lose control.

There are good grayling on the Eden as well, but perhaps the real beauty of this river is the wild browns that average something in the region of twelve ounces, but can grow to three or four pounds or even more. Some of the most dramatic fly fishing I've had in my entire life has been on the Eden, as the summer shadows stretch over the pools and dusk falls in this beautiful part of the world. At times, it's as though the river, which has appeared barren during the day, literally boils with fish. Big fish. Fish cartwheeling out of the water. And, from time to time, there's the tremendous roar of a salmon stimulated by the cooling air. Magnificent memories. If you can, you should make a point of investigating both of these marvellous waters.

TICKETS – my own favourite area of the Eden is centred on Appleby-in-Westmoreland, Cumbria. The Tufton Arms on 01768 351593 can arrange fishing and is situated very close to the river. The management is heavily into fishing as well. Try also the Sandford Arms on 01768 351121, which has private fly fishing for guests on over five miles of double bank water. For the Till, try Brian Thompson, River Keeper, Redscar Cottage, Milfield, Wooler, Northumberland NE71 6JQ on 01668 216223. Or the Estate Office, Ford, Berwick-on-Tweed, on 01890 820224. The Tilmouth Park Hotel, Cornhill-on-Tweed, TD12 4UU can also provide fishing on the Till with its junction on the Tweed. The hotel also offers tremendous salmon fishing for residents. Phone 01890 882255 for details. Prices for both rivers depend on the season and the target fish. Obviously salmon fishing costs more than trout and grayling.

DIRECTIONS – you will find Appleby on the A66 between Penrith and Barnard Castle. The Till runs into the River Tweed close to Cornhill.

ACCOMMODATION – for various kinds of accommodation to be found in the area contact the Tourist Information Centres in Penrith on 01768 867466 or Barnard Castle on 01833 690909. For the River Till area, call the Centre at Coldstream on 01890 882607.

COLDINGHAM LOCH – NORTHUMBERLAND

Perched right on the cliffs between Eyemouth and Dunbar, this is a jewel of a place. Its twenty-two acres give around a mile of bankside fishing – so there's always room to enjoy some seclusion. You can hear, see and smell the ocean. It's a mixture of barren upland and fertile, seductive woodland. Set in a small country estate called Westloch, you can sense it's an ancient place. The estate provides an ideal centre for naturalists, walkers and those who simply want to relax and enjoy unspoilt surroundings. There are also prehistoric hill forts and settlements of archaeological interest nearby.

The loch itself is similarly fascinating. It's deep, generally crystal clear and burgeoning with fertility. Perhaps rare in a loch so far north, annual and frequent weed cutting needs to take place. The owner of the loch, Dr Wise, stresses that this very high water quality makes for some special fishing. In the first place – browns and rainbows – are nearly always in absolutely first-class condition. Great care goes into the stocking policies – generally fish of one and a half to two pounds – and they grow on well in such a friendly environment. In fact, over-wintered rainbows of three and four pounds are commonplace, as are brown trout ranging anything up to six pounds. The fish also fight spectacularly hard: their condition, their almost inevitably perfect fins and the deep, clear water obviously all prove to be stimulating.

The clear, fertile waters of Coldingham Loch also produce fish that are generally only to be caught on imitative patterns. Some small reservoir lures do take fish, but the general visitor prefers to fish more cunningly than that.

Throughout the season, buzzers work very well – especially near evening on a warm, muggy day. All patterns seem to work but it's best to have a good selection with you. Dry flies, too, prove popular. Daddy longleg patterns, sedge patterns, dry hoppers and even caenis imitations throughout June.

In April and May, sunshine leads to an explosion of terrestrial patterns and an eternally rising stock of fish. However, as the heat of the summer progresses, both browns and especially rainbows tend to go deeper. It's now that a floating line with a very long leader and small, weighted nymphs really come into their own. (This is how I personally have been successful at Coldingham – often with leaders in excess of twenty feet in length.) Dr Wise also advises the use of a silver Invictor as a dropper on a two-fly leader. It pays to work the nymph, perhaps a goldhead or something similar, as slowly as possible, keeping an eagle eye open for a very quick jabbing take.

Coldingham, perched so close to the sea, is very much ruled by weather conditions. Strong, cold north-easterlies are not particularly good, nor are bright, calm days in the height of the summer. Ideal is the day with light winds and overcast skies, but even then Coldingham won't offer up its fish easily. Be warned: those of you accustomed to easy put and take stew ponds will find this most beautiful water a tad of a challenge. It's probably fair to say that you need six or seven visits before you can confidently begin to say that you're getting the hang of this charming, characterful loch.

Dr Wise's top tips: it pays to keep on the move and to try different areas until fish can be located. Even on a small water, the trout can be localised and it pays to search until they're found. The other bonus with Coldingham is that Dr Wise is on hand each and every day to impart his expert and deep knowledge of the water.

☙ SEASON – the brown trout season runs from 15 March to 6 October, whilst the rainbow trout season runs from 15 March to 31 October.

🦋 TICKETS – these are bought in advance from Dr E. J. Wise on 01890 771270. A day ticket with a four-fish limit costs £26 from a boat and £21 from the bank. An evening ticket with a three-fish limit is £22 from a boat and £17 from the bank. Boat charges are £4 and £3 respectively, extra per fishing rod. It's important to note that day tickets are by advance booking only as numbers are strictly regulated.

🐟 RULES – single hooks only, no larger than a size 10. These must be barbless or de-barbed if you intend to return fish to the water. There is a twelve-inch minimum takeable size limit and all undersized fish should be returned very carefully. High standards of behaviour are expected at Coldingham as it is a wildlife reserve.

→ DIRECTIONS – taking the A1 north from Berwick-upon-Tweed, turn off onto the A1107 signposted for Eyemouth. Follow the road through Eyemouth and you will come to Coldingham village. Staying on the A1107, leave the village going north towards Edinburgh and turn right immediately at the school, heading towards the coast. This road is not signposted. It is a narrow single-track lane, a no-through road with passing places. This will bring you to Westloch House, the estate and the loch itself. You are asked to drive slowly and carefully along the Westloch road.

🛏 ACCOMMODATION – there is much bed and breakfast and guesthouse accommodation in the area but why not stay on the estate itself in one of the delightful lodges, cottages or chalets? These offer self-catering accommodation of the very highest standard and, for the fisherman, they provide the added bonus of being on the water itself.

❧ HIGHLY RECOMMENDED FISHERIES ❧

- *Tewit Fields, Nr. Carnforth, Lancs. Phone 01524 730331 for details. Seven acres. Good-conditioned, well-sized fish.*
- *Watendlath Tarn, Cumbria. One of Britain's most gorgeous waters. Stunning browns. Highly recommended.*
- *Wykeham Trout Lake, Scarborough, North Yorkshire. Three lakes, all with different levels of challenge. Interesting fishing.*
- *Kielder Reservoir, Northumberland. Call 01434 240398 for details. Two thousand seven hundred acres. Heavily stocked. Stunning surroundings.*
- *Langley Dam, Northumberland. Call 01434 688846 for details. An attractive fishery. Fishing closes in November.*

Fly-Fishing Sites in Scotland

1. Rosslynlee Fishery
2. The Isle of Bute
3. Carron Valley Reservoir
4. Loch Leven
5. Lindores Loch
6. Loch Awe
7. Lochs Laidon, Ericht & Rannoch
8. The River Tummel
9. Lintrathen Loch
10. The River Dee
11. The River Garry

12. Upper River Garry System
13. South Uist
14. The River Spey
15. Stoneyfield Lochs
16. The River Cassley
17. The Rivers Inver & Kirkaig and Loch Assynt
18. Scourie Hill Lochs
19. Tongue Hill Lochs
20. The Shetland Trout Lochs

‛You have tramped the glen and climbed the hill, the sun is hot on your back and the air is heather sweet. Warm from the exertion, you sight at last the loch of your dreams glittering temptingly between the rolling crest. At the water's edge, you pause to drink in the tranquil beauty of it all before the splash of a trout stirs you into action. Fish are cruising the margins in search of their prey and if you cast later, the first trout of the day snatches your Pennel. As you slip it back, its golden flanks wink at you signalling better to come. Right now, this is paradise and there is no finer place to be.'

LESLIE CRAWFORD, RENOWNED HILL LOCH GUIDE AND AUTHOR

Leslie highlights just one aspect of what Scotland has to offer the fly fisherman but there is much, much more. North of the border is just about everything that a fly rod was built for: mighty salmon rivers and wee trout-rich burns; pocket handkerchief lochans, and lochs the size of inland seas; immaculately-run commercial fisheries and completely wild lakes; salmon, grilse, ferox trout, brown trout, sea trout, rainbow trout, grayling and char. The mountainous valleys of the west and the rolling plains of the east, beautiful, peaceful and unspoiled. Indeed, for anyone to say they know everything about Scottish fly fishing would be nonsense. I hope this brief guide to Scottish waters gives you some indication of what you can expect to find in this most glorious of settings.

Just a quick mention of char here. They are present in almost all the deep lochs and are generally unfished. They do, however, come to the surface on warm, summer evenings and can be spotted dimpling around the margins in shallower areas. Very small dry flies or nymphs can pick up these beautiful fish. On lochs where there are fish cages, such as Loch Garry, some of the char have grown large on pellets and can be contacted on spinners and plugs. These fish can be in excess of five pounds.

ROSSLYNLEE FISHERY

Rosslynlee is an enchanting, intimate trout fishery in its own right but especially important because it is so close to Edinburgh, lying just twenty-five miles due south from the city centre. It's a beautiful water, nestling quietly amongst arable land, with stunning views of the Pentland hills stretching out to the west and the Moorfoot range to the south. In fact, a more enticing gateway to the Scottish borders could barely be imagined.

Rosslynlee is a water for all manner of fishing: at just on seven acres, it's not too large to be daunting for beginners and yet still offers a sizeable challenge for the more experienced game fishermen. Given its lush, rural surroundings, Rosslynlee is also large enough to provide peace and serenity for those who want more than just a hooped rod.

High summer can be a problem with over-abundant weed growth and stale, warm water, but not here. Rosslynlee is spring-fed and this maintains water level and clarity whilst also helping to keep temperatures stable. Perhaps this explains why the feeding in the lochan is so prolific with midge, caddis, snails, daphnia, olives and fry all present in abundance. This obviously makes the water ideal for the imitative approach and, not surprisingly, buzzer and dry-fly fishing are both particularly popular during the warmer months. Lure fishing – always favoured by beginners is, however, successful year round and especially so through the colder winter period.

Gilbert Scott, the owner of the fishery, prides himself on the quality of the fish he stocks. These average at least two pounds in weight, with much bigger ones also introduced. But best of all – these are fully finned fish in prime condition. Apart from rainbow trout, which make up the majority of the stocks, there are also brown trout along with some golden and blue trout – always a welcome addition to the basket.

So, if you are holidaying in the borders or making your way up to the city of Edinburgh, this is the perfect stop-over for a few hours of peace and quiet in magnificent surroundings.

SEASON – Rosslynlee is open all the year round. Tuition is offered by Gilbert Scott, a former Scottish international fly fisherman.

TICKETS – contact Gilbert Scott, the owner, at Rosslynlee Trout Fishery, New Biggin Hill, Penicuik, Midlothian, Scotland or phone him on 01968 679606. Tickets cost £22 for a day, four-fish limit. Half-day and evening tickets are £14, with two-fish limits. You can continue to catch and release trout after securing your limit providing you are using small flies only.

DIRECTIONS – you will find Rosslynlee just south-west of Edinburgh near Penicuik. It's on the A6094 between Howgate and Rosewell. The fishery is well-signposted.

ACCOMMODATION – there is accommodation available on site, but phone in plenty of time to assure a booking.

THE ISLE OF BUTE

I love the Isle of Bute simply because it feels like the Highlands and yet it's
so easily accessible from the city of Glasgow. In fact, just an hour or so after
leaving the M8 you can feel yourself entering another world. And that's
what it's like fishing two remarkable waters on the island – Loch Fad and
Loch Quien. These are very different types of water even though they are so
close together. Fad gives more of an impression of a highland water, a bit
more rugged, somewhat more steeply-sided. Quien, on the other hand, is
more low- lying and gives the impression of greater fertility. Both, however,
offer great and exciting challenges.

Fad is the deeper loch and although it can be approached from the bank,
it is probably better tackled by boat – and there is a fleet of thirty on the
water. Typical loch-style tactics work well on this long, thin loch, which is a
mile and three quarters long and a hundred and seventy-five acres in extent.
Never be afraid to ask for the most up-to-the-minute information at the
bailiff's hut, where you will meet with the friendliest advice imaginable.

❧ DEALING WITH GHILLIES ❧

*It's your first time in Scotland, you've forked out for a top beat and
you're to meet the hoary old ghilly by the salmon hut at ten. Help!*
- *Don't be intimidated. It's very easy to almost feel that you have no right
  to be on the river. Remember you're paying him to help.*
- *On the other hand, don't be patronising and overbearing. Remember it's
  important to build up a good relationship.*
- *It's only sense to confess your weaknesses from the outset. If you try to
  hide anything or pretend you're an expert, he'll soon see through you.*
- *Ask for help with your weak areas, whatever they are. A good ghilly will
  always advise and teach conscientiously.*
- *Always do what your ghilly advises – at least for the first few days until
  you have ideas of your own. Remember that he is going to know that
  stretch of the river a thousand times better than you can ever do.*
- *Don't blame the ghilly for your own mistakes. If you miss or lose a fish,
  be brave enough to admit your fault.*
- *Remember that there's nothing like a pint or two in the evening to build
  up rapport. A bit of bonding gets the best out of the day to come.*
- *Remember that salmon fishing is unpredictable. Don't blame your ghilly
  if the fishing is hard or there are very few fish in the river.*

Quien is a quieter water, very beautiful, but the fish are easily spooked. There are only four boats on this ninety-acre loch and all without outboards – something that speaks for itself. In fact, you can approach Quien quite happily from the bank. Near the boathouse there are large areas of water only two to four feet deep and stalking fish here is a distinct possibility. Lures do work but this is very much a nymph water as well. The fish benefit from a rich larder, so shrimp, beetle and corixa patterns are all favourites.

In short, these beautiful lochs offer a typical highland far-away trouting experience and yet lie only an hour or so from the hurly-burly of Glasgow.

SEASON – Quien, a wild and stocked brown trout water, is open from 15 March to 16 October. This water is strictly fly fishing only. Loch Fad, offering both rainbows and browns, is open for fly fishing from 1 March to 17 December and for bait fishing and spinning from 15 March to 6 October. Note that bait and lure fishermen can only operate from the bank.

TICKETS – these are available from Loch Fad Fisheries Limited, Loch Fad, Isle of Bute PA20 9PA. Phone them on 01700 504871. Ticket prices for Loch Quien are £9 a day and for Loch Fad, £15 a day. It's advisable to book boats. These cost £12 a day on a weekday and £14 for the weekend. Tackle is available from the bailiff's hut and fly-fishing rods are for hire, which can be handy if you are visiting in the middle of a business trip, for example.

DIRECTIONS – the mainland ferry terminal at Wemyss Bay on the Clyde coast is easily reached from Glasgow along the M8, turning on to the A73 at Greenock. From Wemyss Bay, the crossing to Rothesay takes a mere thirty minutes by ferry, which operates on a frequent daily service. The waters are around about a mile from the town centre of Rothesay. They are well-signposted along the A845. It is worth noting that a taxi will also take you to the water for a modest fare. It's worth phoning the fishery to book in advance.

ACCOMMODATION – Rothesay itself has a huge number of hotels, guesthouses and bed and breakfast possibilities. Contact the Isle of Bute Tourist Information Centre on 01700 502151 for up-to-the-minute advice on vacancies in your price bracket.

CARRON VALLEY RESERVOIR

Carron Valley Reservoir is situated in the Strathclyde hills near Denny in the east of Scotland. It's a lovely place to fish – one thousand acres of water ringed by wooded hills and spectacular views in every direction. It's a wild, rugged water and the sense of isolation is probably increased by the fact that bank fishing is not allowed. All you'll see during the course of the day is an abundance of wildlife and a few boats dotted here and there, but never with a sense of overcrowding.

The brown trout fishing is quite excellent and though the fish average just under a pound, several between four and six pounds are taken each year.

Although it's a large water, Carron Valley responds very well to buzzers of various sizes, more typical flies such as the Gold Butcher or Bibio, as well as the Black Pennel, the Soldier Palmer or dry flies when the water warms up.

Have no fear, there are plenty of fish. There is an outstanding stock of wild browns but the Carron Valley staff also stock around four thousand trout per season, usually introduced on a fortnightly basis. The staff, you'll find, are extremely helpful, pointing you in all the right directions.

Season – boat fishing only, April to September.
Tickets – contact Fraser McGowan on 01324 823698 or visit www.carronvalley.com. A bank permit costs £10, with a three-fish limit and catch and release thereafter. Boat hire prices vary, one day's hire including outboard, fuel and two permits costs £33.
Facilities – toilets, fishing lodge, disabled facilites, car parking, outboard hire and lifejackets. There are sixteen boats on the water, four at eighteen feet and twelve at fifteen feet. Lifejackets are supplied, which must be worn.
Directions – Carron Valley Reservoir is situated in the Carron Valley by Denny FK6 RJL. It is well-signposted.

Loch Leven – Perth and Kinross

Loch Leven has probably had more words written about it than any other trout water in Britain, certainly in Scotland. For decades now its special strain of brown trout has been revered and much transported to other waters. There's something special about Leven: it's very large – three thousand five hundred acres – feels remote and yet is uniquely accessible. In fact, it's just north of the great cities of Scotland, hardly a stone's throw off the M90 and yet, when you're out there in your boat it's another world.

I can't pretend that I've ever done any better than moderately well on Leven: it's a water that really does respond to local knowledge and experience but, having said that, I've never ever regretted a single moment spent on its waters. I'm sure it will get you like that: there's something totally magical about it and even if you only have a moderate bag compared with the experts, I can guarantee you'll still have the time of your life.

Leven is a fascinating water of varying depths, bottom contours and dotted by islands. What's more you can fish late – anything up to 11.30pm in the evening at the peak of the summer – and that gives it a truly magical feel. Potter back to the pier in the half-light with the fish still rising around you, and you'll know you've been a part of something very special.

Both the browns and the splendidly fighting rainbows respond to the notorious moods of Leven, so it pays to ring the changes during the course of the day. During good weather, it's most exciting to fish buzzers and dry

111

flies on the surface and really see the action, but there are times that you'll have to use sinking lines to get deeper. The answer is to be adaptable and, if you are, you'll really make the most of this spell-binding water.

☀ SEASON – 20 March to 6 October.

🎏 TICKETS – these are available from the pier in Kinross, on the water itself. Day permits cost £30 for a boat with a maximum of three rods. Evening permits vary between £24 and £30, again for three rods. There is no bag limit on browns over ten inches and you're allowed to take twelve rainbows.

👕 FACILITIES – there is a café, toilets, telephones and tackle hire.

→ DIRECTIONS – take the M90 north and turn off at junction 6. The water is well-signposted.

🛏 ACCOMMODATION – the Roxburghe Guesthouse, 126, High Street, Kinross KY13 7DA is very convenient for the water. Phone 015778 629498 for details.

LINDORES LOCH – FIFE

This is a lovely Scottish water of around ninety-five acres, averaging around eight feet in depth. It is a fertile water and the fact that the loch is so shallow encourages fish to take from the surface. In fact, buzzer patterns are particularly recommended, especially once the water begins to warm up. Most of the fish are rainbows, but they are in excellent condition and average two pounds or above. By the way, there are also stocks of excellent perch sometimes topping three pounds.

This is a particularly beautiful water and fishes very well on warm, still evenings. Also watch out for such rarities as the occasional passing osprey.

But, whatever, remember to pack those buzzers, particularly in olive, claret and black. Nymphs, however, are also taken in this water, along with traditionals such as an Invicta Wickham's.

☀ SEASON – March to the end of November.

🎏 TICKETS – contact Andy Mitchell on 01337 810488 or write to him at The Fishing Hut, Lindores Loch, By Newburgh, Fife KY14 6JB. A two-man boat costs £36. Ten fish allowed per boat. A three-man boat costs £45, with fifteen fish allowed per boat. For a single angler, subject to availability, £18 with a five-fish limit. Catch and release is allowed after the limit is taken on de-barbed hooks.

⚖ RECORDS – 11lb 8oz rainbow, 5lb 8oz brown.

👕 FACILITIES – Toilets. Lodge with seating, cooker, free tea and coffee, sale of fly patterns, tuition, electric outboard hire.

→ DIRECTIONS – from Edinburgh, come north on the M90, turning right at junction 8 and taking the A91 Cupar–St. Andrews road. Turn left onto the B937, signposted Newburgh. The loch is two miles along this road on the left-hand side.

Loch Awe – Argyll

I'm going to talk unreservedly now about one of my great passions – ferox fishing. The ferox is the mighty, Scottish predatorial trout, and it has been a great favourite with anglers for well over a century now, ever since the trolling style of fishing, pioneered by Victorian sportsmen. There are those that say that trolling is boring but I cannot agree with them. It's exhilarating to be out on a grand day in a beautiful loch such as Awe, with its spectacular views. Take binoculars with you and you will be sure to see some magnificent bird life, and perhaps even some deer as they come to drink at the water's edge as the dusk pulls in.

And what fish these ferox are. You won't find anything like them anywhere else in the world – big, bold, brilliantly coloured. Of course, trolling is a specialised art but there are books on the subject, and perhaps you've already done some. Certainly, my advice if you're heading to Scotland is to stick in a spinning rod and some lures and you'll be halfway there.

Awe is justly famous for its huge ferox – fish of over twenty-five pounds exist in this mysterious loch. But there are also other fine trout to be taken on fly as well. Mostly the 'normal' trout weigh around half a pound or so but there are better fish of at least double that weight to be taken on the fly.

Just a word or two about safety: always wear a lifejacket, always take oars, make sure you have a reliable engine and plenty of fuel. Let people know your course and estimated time of return, and don't go out in stormy weather or if there's a bad weather forecast. In short, never take any risks whatsoever. A ferox is a mighty prize indeed but not one worth dying for!

My favourite months are March to early June, and then September, but there are times when high summer can prove very productive.

Season – the annual close season for trout extends from 7 October to 14 March, both days included.

Tickets – the Loch Awe Improvement Association sells season, weekly and daily tickets and these can be found in hotels, Post Offices and tackle shops throughout Scotland. They can also be obtained from from D. Wilson, Ardbrecknish House, Dalmally, PA33 1AQ. Boats and permits can also be bought from the Taycreggan Hotel, Kilchrenan, by Taynuilt, Argyle PA35 1HQ on 01866 833211, the Cuil-na-sithe Hotel on 01866 833234 and the Sonachan Hotel, Port Sonachan, by Dalmally, Argyle PA33 1BN on 01866 833240. Also contact Mr. N. D. Clark, 11 Dalavich, by Taynuilt on 01866 844209.

Directions – take the A82 to Tyndrum and from there the A85 on to Dalmally at the head of the loch.

Accommodation – any of the hotels named above. The Taycreggan Hotel has my personal recommendation. It is situated right on the loch side with its own jetty and fishing fleet. An excellent experience.

LOCHS LAIDON, ERICHT AND RANNOCH – INVERNESSHIRE

There is a remarkable cluster of lochs, just to the west of Pitlochry, set in some of the most dramatic of Scottish scenery. Between them, Ericht, Rannoch and Laidon have produced extraordinary numbers of both ferox trout and normal brown trout. These are very wild places to fish, and not for the timid, but the rewards can be excellent. So beautiful is the scenery that even a fish-less day is no hardship. Trolling is practised on all three lochs but it's also possible to catch excellent trout on traditional fly tactics, simply drifting with the wind and fishing a team of flies close to the surface.

There are other bonuses. Try, for example, the River Gaur that links Laidon to Rannoch. This is a mesmerising, tumultuous river full of wicked rapids and deep, slow pools. Once again, it's the home of many trout and some earth-shattering ferox. In short, if you fancy something on the wild side, think hard about a journey up to this spellbinding part of Scotland.

SEASON – the closed season for trout is 7 October to 14 March inclusive.

TICKETS – The Loch Rannoch Conservation Association has fishing on Loch Rannoch and the local shops and hotels sell permits. For Loch Ericht, permits are available from the Loch Ericht Hotel, Dalwhinnie, Invernesshire PH14 1AF. Phone 01528 522257 for details. A day permit is £9.50 and boats are available to hire. For Loch Laidon and the River Gaur, contact the Moor of Rannoch Hotel, Rannoch Station PH17 2QA on 01882 633238. Tickets are £9.50 per rod. The local tackle shop, The Country Store, Kinlochrannoch, Perthshire is also a fund of information.

DIRECTIONS – for Rannoch and Laidon, take the A9 north of Pitlochry. After eight miles, turn off left on the B847 Kinlochrannoch. Follow the picturesque B846 as far as it goes to Rannoch Station, way out on Rannoch moor. Loch Laidon can be found further to the west. For Dalwhinnie, continue up the A9 turning off left on the A889.

ACCOMMODATION – the Moor of Rannoch Hotel, Rannoch Station is one of the most dramatic outposts any angler will ever come across. The Ericht Hotel also has a fine feroxing reputation! See above for details.

THE RIVER TUMMEL – PERTHSHIRE

The River Tummel in and around Pitlochry offers some wonderful rough-water trout and grayling fishing. Most of the beats are controlled by the Pitlochry Angling Club, which affords some tremendous opportunities for visiting anglers. Brown trout fishing opens on 15 March and is fly only to 30 June. Bait from then onwards , until the trout fishing finishes on 6 October. However, grayling fishing specifically opens on 7 October and continues until 14 March. So, you see, fishing is pretty well all year round.

Trout fishing is probably at its best in the late spring and summer with some tremendous hatches taking place in the early evening. Moreover, the trout are browns and in beautiful condition.

It's for the grayling fishing, though, that many people come this far. These really are grayling as God originally made them! There are some very big fish indeed, and two pounders aren't unusual. These deep, heavily-shouldered fish, with brilliant deep blue colouring, can be taken on both fly and bait. Look also for the deeper streamier runs. It pays to keep moving, searching different lies until a group of grayling is contacted. Fun can then be fast and furious, but use barbless hooks so they can be slipped back with ease.

SEASON – trout and grayling fishing 15 March to 6 October; grayling fishing 7 October to 14 March.

TICKETS – £5 per day and £15 per week for both trout and grayling. Tickets are available from from Pitlochry Tourist Information Centre on 01796 472215. For season tickets, apply to the club secretary on 01796 472484.

DIRECTIONS – the fishing is generally through Pitlochry town and on the outskirts. It is wise to visit Mitchells' tackle shop and look closely at the map for the proper beats.

ACCOMMODATION – Pitlochry offers a wealth of bed and breakfasts, guesthouses and hotels. The Pitlochry Tourist Information Centre on 01796 472215 can provide you with phone numbers.

LINTRATHEN LOCH – ANGUS

This is a really stunning water, not that far north of Dundee, but a great place to get away from it all. The lovely thing about Lintrathen is the immaculately conditioned brown trout, many of them wild but with stocks judiciously topped up with quality fish. Fishing is by boat and because of the loch's size, you can easily get away from company if you fancy fishing on your own. A lot of the water is ringed by rhododendron bushes and the roots and overhanging branches attract a good number of fish. Also, look around the rocky shorelines and the dam for bigger fish.

Most Lintrathen browns average around twelve ounces to a pound and a half, but two pound plus fish are quite common, with a very few going to double figures. But it's not size that attracts anglers back again and again to this charming water: it's the views, the quality of the fishing and the feeling of spaciousness.

Top wet flies are the Bibio, the Black Pennel and Black Spider. Try Black Hoppers and Black Buzzers for evening rises. A last tip: stick to the margins, where the majority of the natural food is to be found. This is a working reservoir with very deep, comparatively sterile water out in the middle.

⛅ **SEASON** – first weekend in April to first Sunday in October.

✦ **TICKETS** – Boats are £36 and this includes the outboard motor along with fuel. There's a ten-fish boat limit. Please phone Mr. Yule for prior booking (see below).

✦ **CONTACT** – Jack Yule on 01575 560327 or 01575 573816. Lintrathen Angling Club, The Boathouse Lodge, Lintrathen Reservoir, by Alyth.

✦ **RECORDS** – the heaviest recorded brown weighed 11lb 4oz, but 3lb is considered an excellent fish.

✦ **FACILITIES** – there are toilets and an anglers' shelter along with weighing facilities but don't expect smart clubhouses, refreshments and so on. It's not that kind of fishery.

➡ **DIRECTIONS** – Lintrathen lies to the north of the A926 Alyth–Kirriemuir road. Turn off the A926 onto the B954, signposted Glenisla. You pass a couple of golf courses and then turn right, following this road past the Reekie Lin – which is a series of waterfalls – past the turn off for Backwater Reservoir until you come to the Lintrathen Anglers' car park.

THE RIVER DEE – ABERDEENSHIRE

The River Dee is another of Scotland's classic salmon rivers, justifiably so. Indeed, for many anglers, the Dee is the epitome of a fly river with endless pools just built for the job. Most of my time on the Dee has been in the Spring when fly fishing has been something of a chore. But on one notable occasion I had a week in the summer when there were fish around, when the water was low and clear and you could really get in tune with the fish.

It's not particularly hard to catch salmon in perfect conditions, when the river is at a good level and the fish are teeming. It's much harder when the water is low, clear and warm, and under such conditions an angler really has to fish skilfully. Try using a floating line and a small black fly. Work your way down the pool, casting twice from each stance then dropping a couple of paces down river before casting again. Put your fly across the river and slightly downstream so it works across in a steady movement. Visualise your fly working some six or eight inches beneath the surface and concentrate hard. If you do get a take, don't necessarily expect a hard tug – sometimes all you'll feel is a tweak or see a gleam of silver. The great days on the Dee, like any other salmon river, come when the rain has fallen but that doesn't mean to say that you can't have great fun in the warmer months too.

⛅ **SEASON** – early February to 1 November

✦ **TICKETS** – the Dee, as you'd expect, is very difficult to get fishing on. Its beats are highly-prized. However, rods are sometimes available from the Factor, Invercauld Estates Office, Braemar, by Ballater AB3 5TR on 01339 741224. Also try Glen Tanar Estate, Brooks House, Glen Tanar AB34 5EU on 01339 886451. The Banchory Lodge Hotel, Banchory AB31 3HS, also has salmon and trout fishing on the Dee available for five rods. Phone 01330 822625.

→ **DIRECTIONS** – the Dee runs west from Aberdeen. Banchory and Ballater can both be accessed along the A93. This charming road runs the length of the Dee valley.

⊨ **ACCOMMODATION** – there is a wealth of bed and breakfast and guesthouse accommodation in Banchory, Aboyne and Ballater. The Banchory Lodge Hotel is situated right on the river with a glorious pool outside the dining room windows. It is expensive but comes highly, personally recommended.

THE RIVER GARRY – INVERNESSHIRE

You don't have to go too far back in history to read of a time when the Invernesshire Garry was one of Scotland's most famous salmon waters. Since the 1950s, however, the advent of hydro-electric power has damaged runs of fish to some degree. However, the river is still an absolutely enchanting place to fish and offers very healthy stocks indeed. The river is perhaps at its best from the foot of Loch Garry to the river mouth in Loch Oich. Here you have three and a half miles of spectacular water – a mixture of tumbling falls and open glides amid the most wondrous Scottish scenery.

Although spinning is permitted, the pools are ideal for fly fishing and, once the temperatures begin to rise, it would be a crime to do anything else. Big fish come in early and January can often see salmon in excess of twenty-five pounds. The prime weeks are generally in April and May, but runs of grilse are common later on in the season throughout August and September.

The river is being extremely well looked after – recently the thick rhododendron undergrowth has been cleared somewhat to allow more light on the water and better access for the anglers.

There's also a catch and release policy that plays an integral part in fishery management. Each party may keep one wild salmon each week fished, but all others should be returned. And here's the exciting part: for each fresh fish returned, you're given a whole farmed salmon in its place. What a great idea!

☀ **SEASON** – 15 January to 14 October

✦ **TICKETS** – the fishing is let by the week and information is obtainable from Garry Fishings, c/o Invergarry Hotel, Invergarry, Invernesshire. Phone 01809 501206 for more information. Prices vary according to the popularity of the week.

☀ **ARRANGEMENTS** – fishing is restricted to six rods on any day. Tenants who book an entire week of six rods will have totally exclusive use of all facilities – this includes the spacious fishing cabin with table and chairs, lighting, mains water and sink, microwave oven and conventional cooker with, naturally enough, rod racks. This is situated on the river bank with its own private car park.

→ **DIRECTIONS** – Invergarry is found on the junction of the A87 and the A82, south of Fort Augustus. Fort Augustus is seven miles away and Fort William twenty-five miles.

⊨ **ACCOMMODATION** – the Invergarry Hotel itself on 01809 501206, is a delightful and convenient place to stay, as is its sister hotel the Glengarry Castle, on 01809 501254, situated on the banks of Loch Oich. Self-catering is available at the Old Mill in the village. Phone Kevin Reed on 01207 545538.

UPPER RIVER GARRY SYSTEM – TOMDOUN

Tomdoun is the centre of it all. This extraordinary Highland lodge dates from the late Victorian period and boasts one of the best views of anywhere in the world. Walk outside the Tomdoun, now a cosy fisherman's hotel, and all you will see is mountains and water, all available to residents. Brace yourself – you really are in paradise.

So what is there within a five or six mile radius? Firstly, Loch Quoich – a stunning lunar-type loch up in the mountains where you will see deer and snow on the summits throughout the year. Quoich is a ferox trout loch for those who care to troll and for the fly fisher, a wild brown trout water that can produce twenty or more fish a day averaging around ten to twelve ounces. Fish Quoich traditionally on the drift and as the sun sets and the wind eases, trout will dimple the surface everywhere. You're in wonderland.

Dropping down the valley, back towards the hotel, you come to the wonderful Loch Poulary – minute compared with Quoich's eight miles by a mile. Poulary, by comparison, is a mere two hundred acres or so, and much more friendly to those used to smaller waters. In fact, on Poulary – which is equally as stunning as Quoich in its own way – you can probably use a greater variety of methods. Poulary, somehow, is kinder, cosier than Quoich. You can pick up trout on dry fly, buzzer or nymph, as well as traditional wet patterns. And the trout are generally bigger. Poulary is more lush and fertile and the browns grow on a pace. Fish of one to two pounds are not unusual.

As the Garry system falls out of the tail of Poulary, the river becomes really interesting. Pools and rapids proliferate and at times, especially in the later summer, a good number of salmon work their way upstream. This is super salmon fishing, either with spinner or, preferably, with fly – especially when the water is low and clear. And, as ever, the river is surrounded by landscape so beautiful that you simply have to stop and gawp.

You can work your way down river through three or four miles, past the hotel itself, down to where it enters lovely Loch Inchlaggan – yet another fly fishers' paradise. With an area of around three or four hundred acres, Loch Inchlaggan is shallow apart from the deep central channel. Forty or fifty years ago, the river wound its way through pasture but the dam at Garry raised the waters and Inchlaggan was formed. Like Poulary, Inchlaggan is a warm, fertile sort of water, responsive to all types of fly fishing methods.

And we're not just talking about brown trout fishing here – excellent brown trout at that – but also some fabulous Arctic char have begun to make an appearance. Many of these are big fish: expect three, four, or even five pounders! And they can be caught on the fly – honestly! Try brown nymphs, tied on a size eight or ten, fished deep and slow over six to ten feet of water. Don't be in too much of a hurry to move – the char shoals can drift in and out day long. Of course, I'm not guaranteeing that you'll catch one of these super char but to do so, I promise, is a thrill of a lifetime.

Inchlaggan opens out into Loch Garry proper – another famous ferox water. Trout fishing in traditional fashion is also very popular and fish of one to two pounds are frequent. Then, rod weary, it's back to the Tomdoun for a bath, a meal, a bar-side chat and bed. The perfect fisherman's inn, Tomdoun.

🐟 SEASON – the trout fishing runs from 17 March to 6 October. Salmon fishing opens in January and runs until 14 October.

🎣 TICKETS – Loch Quoich is boat fishing only and the hotel has two boats on it. Loch Poulary is also boat fishing only and boats can be booked from the hotel. Lochs Inchlaggan and Garry are best fished by boat but bankside permits can also be bought for here. Boats cost £30 per day with an engine and £14 each day if you bring your own. Day tickets for the bank are £3. The river itself can only be fished by hotel residents whereas the lochs are open to all comers.

→ DIRECTIONS – to find Tomdoun, follow the A82 from Fort William north-west towards Fort Augustus. At Invergarry, turn left on the A87, signposted to Skye. The signs to the Tomdoun Hotel can be found in around four miles, on the left-hand side of the road. The narrow track will take you past Loch Garry to the hotel itself, on the right.

🛏 ACCOMMODATION – the Tomdoun Hotel can be contacted on 01809 511244.

🎓 OTHER CONSIDERATIONS – never go out on the water without a lifejacket, especially on Loch Quoich. Never take more fish than you personally are going to need to eat. The Tomdoun waters are run very carefully with conservation in mind.

SOUTH UIST – HEBRIDES

It's not often that I would think of including a whole island as one single entry, but such is the profusion of fishing in South Uist that I think we can really go for it here! The definitive guide is written by John Kennedy and is called, aptly enough, simply *Seventy Lochs*! South Uist is a haven for the brown trout fly fisherman. There is no other word to use. It can seem that round every bend in the road there is yet another enticing water to fish. I've only been fortunate enough to cast a fly on three or four of them – merely scraping the surface – but those few outings have lived with me even though they took place now some fifteen or so years back.

The great thing about South Uist fishing is the quality of the brown trout. On many, if not most, of the lochs, the browns – all wild and spirited – average at least a pound in weight and that's quite some size for lochs of this nature. Quantity is not the issue, but that won't stop a reasonably competent fly fisherman getting more than his fair share during a serious day's outing. And what's more, you're almost certain to be on your own. It's like owning your own waters – waters that are either free or ridiculously inexpensive.

As you'd expect on a Western Isle, wind is generally with you. This can help keep midges away and it certainly does help mask a fly line. Flies not to be without include the Soldier Palmer, the Black Penal, Blue Zulu, Peter Ross, Invictor, Grouse and Claret, all the Butcher patterns, the Green French Partridge, the Claret Bumble and the Golden Olive Bumble. At least that's what John Kennedy advises, and who would argue with him? Oh, and as Mr Kennedy says, there's no real need for gossamer-light tippets. He suggests leaders of six-pounds breaking strain and he could well be right – don't forget that four- and even five-pound browns are always a real possibility.

Sea trout have been holding up well on South Uist as well, and later in the year there are good runs of salmon – especially grilse. Sea trout can easily top the six- or seven-pound mark and they come in good numbers. Still, it has to be said that it is the brown trout fishing that makes South Uist so special, the browns that lure dedicated anglers back to the island. That and the island's sublime beauty of course. Its loneliness. Its unspoilt loveliness.

☀ SEASON – brown trout 1 April to 30 September. June is probably seen as the prime month. Sea trout and salmon really begin in July and finish at the end of October.

⚡ TICKETS – the fishing rights on most waters in South Uist are owned by the South Uist Estate with the exception of a handful of lochs that are reserved for guests of the estate itself and the Lochboisdale Hotel. The estate has let the fishing rights to the South Uist Angling Club, which issues permits on a daily or weekly basis. These can be obtained from the secretary of the club, from Bornish General Stores in Bornish itself and from Colin Campbell Sports, Balivanich, Benbecula on 01870 602236. Tickets to many lochs are also available from the Lochboisdale Hotel on 01878 700332.

➔ DIRECTIONS – South Uist can be reached by ferry from Oban or Mallaig. Both dock at Lochboisdale. British Airways also run flights to the island. Phone 01870 602310 for details. There is car hire available locally. As for the lochs themselves, it's hard to miss them – especially with Kennedy's guide.

🛏 ACCOMMODATION – there is bed and breakfast availability around the island but most serious anglers understandably head for the Lochboisdale Hotel itself (details above). This is the centre of angling activity on the island – as it has been for many, many years. The hotel offers boats, ghillies, and the most up-to-the-minute advice on the best lochs, the best flies and the best methods. A classic Scottish angling hotel and highly recommended.

Traditional char fishing on Lake Windermere demands vastly long rods and lines hundreds of metres long, decorated with scores of tiny silver spinners. It's a difficult art form, but immensely enjoyable.

The River Tay remains one of Scotland's premier salmon rivers, and big fish still ascend it year after year. A beautiful, historic water, and one that every fly fisher should attempt to visit.

Scotland isn't all about rushing majestic rivers, and in the glens you will find beautiful little waters such as this one, the River Lyon, hidden away from tourist and angler alike.

If it's a challenge you want then you can't beat a vast water like Loch Ness. You can troll it for salmon and ferox or simply take a boat out and fish for trout using the traditional loch method.

Salmon fishing in Scotland is often a lonely, waiting game. It pays to be up early, especially when the water is low and clear, as salmon will often take more confidently before the light grows.

The loughs of Northern Ireland really are a paradise for both game and coarse fishermen. You'll frequently find pike, bream, rudd, trout and salmon within the one water system. Sport for all.

Richie Johnson with a magnificent Lough Mask wild brown. Just look at the vivid spotting and the immaculate fins. No wonder this dearest of friends looks so pleased.

The wild trout of Ireland fight like no other fish on these or any other shores. The gin-clear water, the fabulously rich diet of insects and the spirit of the Irish means that your rod will be long bent.

THE RIVER SPEY – INVERNESSHIRE

The River Spey is one of the classic Scottish salmon rivers, a joy to fish and running through some spectacular Scottish countryside. Of course, in common with all Scottish rivers, stocks have been variable over the past years, but there is every evidence that the situation is on the mend now – perhaps in part because the net fishing ceased at the end of the 1993 season and there is now no commercial netting for salmon within the Spey district.

The Spey is a largely unspoilt river with next to no pollution and it's a water made for fly fishing. In the past, my own favourite time of the year has been late April into early May, although later on in the year runs of grilse can pack the river and make for very exciting sport – especially on a floating line and small fly.

Naturally enough, many beats of the Spey are difficult to get a rod upon but there are some opportunities, and reasonably priced ones at that. Believe me, it's well worth exploration.

SEASON – the salmon and sea trout season runs from 11 February to 30 September and the brown trout season from 15 March to 30 September. Obviously, the Spey is heavily weather-dependent but all things being equal, the best months for salmon appear to be April and May and then August into September towards the end of the season.

TICKETS – the Strathspey Angling Improvement Association has seven miles on the Spey and permits are offered to visitors resident in Grantown, Cromdale and surrounding areas. The Seafield Lodge Hotel, Grantown-on-Spey, PH26 3JN, is an excellent base for anglers. Phone 01479 872152 for details of the fishing. It would be wrong not to mention the late Arthur Oglesby and his world-famous course on the Spey, which is based at Grantown – Arthur was one of the most respected instructors in history and a marvellous man to boot. Moving further up river to Aviemore, the Rothiemurchus Highland Estate also offers both salmon and sea trout fishing on four miles of the Spey. The fishing here is by fly only, though spinning is sometimes allowed in high water conditions. For more details phone 01479 810703. The Abernethy Angling Improvement Association also offers fishing on the Spey at a very reasonable cost. The fishing is centred around the Boat of Garten and Aviemore and comprises nearly ten miles of fishing over many named pools. There is water to suit all types of fishing here from both fast runs to deep, slow stretches. The stretches are available to visitors staying locally in the Boat of Garten and Aviemore areas. Tickets can be obtained from Allens, Deshar Road, Boat of Garten, Invernesshire, PH24 3BN, on 01479 831372. and Speyside Sports, 2 Grampian Road, Aviemore, Invernesshire, PH22 1PD, on 01479 810656.

→ DIRECTIONS – the area is well-served by both the A9 and the A95.

ACCOMMODATION – try the Seafield Lodge Hotel (see above for details). For further accommodation apply to the Highlands of Scotland Tourist Board, Peffery House, Strathpeffer, Ross-shire. Phone them on 01870 5143070 for details.

STONEYFIELD LOCHS – ROSS-SHIRE

The Stoneyfield Loch complex consists of two five-acre lochs for fly fishing only and one three-acre loch for both bait and fly. Although this is largely a rainbow-stocked water, I've included it here because it's such a quiet, attractive fishery, ideal for a club competition or for a picturesque family day out. Furthermore, the calibre of the trout is excellent. The fishery stocks on a weekly basis with real quality rainbows ranging from one and a half up to just into double figures. As an added bonus, there are also a number of natural brown trout in the water. Again, these are beautiful fish.

All usual trout fishing methods work, but don't neglect buzzers and dry flies in comparatively calm, warm conditions. Imitative patterns – nymphs in particular – also work well, so don't be blinded by lures.

Overall, this is a lovely place to stop at and enjoy if you're motoring up the east coast. It's a family-run business and the owners pride themselves on giving customers a friendly greeting and a memorable day's fishing.

SEASON – 1 March to 30 November. Monday to Saturday 9.00am till dusk or 10.00pm whichever is earlier. Sunday 9.00am till 6.00pm.

TICKETS – these can be booked from Stonefield Lochs, Newmore, Invergordon, Ross-shire, on 01349 852632, or e-mail stonefieldloch@talk21.com. Tickets cost £8.50 for two hours, one-fish limit, £14 for four hours, two-fish limit, £18 for six hours, three-fish limit and £23 for eight hours, four-fish limit. Catch and release is possible after the limit's been taken.

FACILITIES – tackle hire is available and flies are for sale. There is a fishing hut with microwave and tea-making facilities. There is a toilet built with the disabled in mind.

DIRECTIONS – Stoneyfield is situated just off the A9, three miles north of Alness and three miles from Invergordon. It is well-signposted.

ACCOMMODATION – bed and breakfast is available at the Ship Inn Guesthouse, 33 Shore Road, Invergordon, Ross-shire IV18 0ER. Phone 01349 852427 for details. The Highlands of Scotland Tourist Board on 0870 5143070 will be able to recommend further accommodation.

THE RIVER CASSLEY – ROSEHALL WATER – SUTHERLAND

I've only had occasional days on the River Cassley but the Rosehall water will stay with me forever. The Cassley is a short river, just ten or twelve miles long, and is a tributary of the more famous Oykel. However, it's not always possible to get on the really classic salmon rivers and opportunities like the Cassley should be grabbed. The fishing is really looking good these days, under the supervision of Hugo Graesser. However, the Cassley offers more than just excellent salmon fishing. This is a truly beautiful, awe-inspiring piece of water that is fished on the fly only. It provides challenging fishing with a wide variety of pools, in settings of outstanding natural beauty. There are waterfalls, gorges and gentle parkland. In fact, the ever-changing backdrop is almost as wonderful as the fishing itself. The fishing is easily accessible by car, so this makes it suitable for older anglers.

There are many salmon rivers in Scotland where it's quite possible to believe that you really are in another magical world, and the Rosehall water is certainly one of these places. It's truly an atmosphere to be savoured and, if you get one of the salmon – as well you might – there's a very big likelihood that it will be covered in sea-lice, always an added bonus.

The management encourages the return of fish and more and more regulars are putting salmon back. We live in a new age that, thankfully, is encouraging the return of these marvellous fish to rivers like the Cassley.

SEASON – April fishing can be very good and grilse appear around June. If there is a reasonable amount of rain in the late summer and autumn – up till the end of September – many fish are expected to run.

TICKETS – contact Hugo Graesser at Rosehall Sportings to discuss vacant weeks. Prior booking is obviously essential as increasing runs of fish are adding to the Cassley's popularity. Prices vary from £750–£900 for three rods, and the services of an experienced ghilly are included.

RULES – the lower Cassley is run as two beats, each for three rods and rotating daily at 1.00pm. Between the two beats there are twenty-nine named and recognised pools and fish can be caught in most levels of water. Fly fishing only.

DIRECTIONS – the Rosehall water is found thirteen miles west of Bonar Bridge on the A37 Lochinver Road.

ACCOMMODATION – anglers on the river tend to stay at the Achness Hotel situated very close to the river. It's a fine fishing hotel with a friendly atmosphere and good cuisine. Seven double bedrooms with private bathrooms. Phone 01549 441239 for details. The Highlands of Scotland Tourist Board, Peffery House, Strathpeffer, Ross-shire, IV14 9HA, on 0870 5143070 can advise on further accommodation in the area.

THE RIVERS INVER AND KIRKAIG AND LOCH ASSYNT – SUTHERLAND

I've grouped these two beautiful rivers and a stunning loch together as they really do form a unique triumvirate. The Inver drains Assynt into a sea loch on the west coast of Sutherland, whilst the Kirkaig is an equally short river just three and a half miles south of Loch Inver. Both rivers have good runs of salmon. Loch Assynt is known for its brown trout, especially the fabled ferox. There are also numerous other hill lochs such as Poll, Drumbeg, Culag and Fionn nearby. All these boast excellent wild brown trout fishing.

This really is a very special area indeed, one of outstanding natural beauty. In fact, to walk the valley of the Kirkaig is an experience in itself and if you're lucky to have a salmon rod under your arm, almost heaven! Of course, as is the way of it these days, runs of salmon are unpredictable and these are spate rivers, so good rainfall is frequently necessary. The fish can be quite large considering the size of the rivers, but the fishing itself is fascinating with all manner of challenging pools.

Loch Assynt is wild and wonderful and offers some excellent brown trout fishing, with occasional monsters of ten pounds or more taken on both fly and lure. To be afloat on Loch Assynt is an experience not to be missed.

I've visited the area many times and have been lucky enough to catch salmon up to twelve pounds and brown trout up to eight pounds on my visits. But it's not really the fish that I will remember, it's more the dramatic scenery and the extraordinary sunsets out across Lochinver harbour. This is a most beautiful part of the fisherman's lovely world.

SEASON – 16 March to 7 October inclusive.

TICKETS – these are not always easily come by but the Inver Lodge Hotel has salmon fishing on three beats of the Inver and further fishing on the Kirkaig. Apply to the Inver Lodge Hotel, Lochinver, IV27 4LU, on 01571 844496. Assynt Angling Club controls twenty-seven hill lochs with excellent brown trout fishing both to the north and east of Lochinver. Tickets are generally between £5 and £6. They are obtainable from the Tourist Office or Simpsons Newsagents, Lochinver. Lochinver Tourist Office also sells tickets for Lochs Poll, Roe, Manse and Tuirk, which still produce sea trout runs. For fishing on Loch Assynt, contact the Inchnadamph Hotel on 01571 822202.

→ DIRECTIONS – Lochinver is found off the Ullapool to Scourie road. Pass Inchnadamph and in a few miles, fork left along the shore of Loch Assynt following the A837 to Lochinver. This is stunning countryside.

ACCOMMODATION – both the Inver Lodge Hotel and Inchnadamph Hotel are highly recommended and well-geared up for fishermen (see above for details). The Highlands of Scotland Tourist Board, Peffery House, Strathpeffer, Ross-shire, IV14 9HA, on 0870 5143070, will be able to recommend further accommodation.

SCOURIE HILL LOCHS – HIGHLANDS

One of the most enchanting times I've ever spent in Scotland was staying at the Scourie Hotel and investigating just a few of the lochs in the hills behind. There is an astonishing profusion of historic waters up here set in extreme remoteness. The Scourie Hotel itself boasts twenty-five thousand acres of brown trout, sea trout and salmon fishing, along with eighteen boats. However, for the trout, all you need is a good pair of walking boots, strong legs and capacious lungs! It is quite possible that if you're really adventurous you will find waters that haven't been fished for a season or more, but don't expect the fish to be easy, or necessarily large. What you're looking at here is really challenging – wild brown trout fishing for specimens of unparalleled beauty. It's never a bad idea to take a compass with you: if a mist comes down it can be difficult to find your way down off the hill. And do remember that what started out as a beautiful day can quickly and easily turn into a wild, wet and windy one.

Waters range from the gin-clear to the dark and the peaty, but as there are limestone outcrops in the vicinity you'll find some waters that are very fertile with much bigger fish. Obviously, ask advice, then strike out and do your own thing. All traditional flies work splendidly but don't forget to stick in some imitative patterns: several nymph patterns, buzzers and some sedge patterns can work wonders. The main thing is to be bold and ring the changes. Never forget to work the margins before you try putting out a longer line. If you're the first on the water for weeks, if not months, you'll often find very big fish cruising in the shallow margins, their dorsals clear of the water. Exciting and very beautiful stuff indeed.

☀ **SEASON** – the trout season runs from 2 April to 7 October. You will only find wild browns in the Scourie Hill Lochs, some salmon and some sea trout.

🎣 **TICKETS** – phone the Scourie Hotel on 01971 502396 for information on day tickets. These start at around £5. Fishing is free to residents at the hotel. The Scourie Angling Club also has rights on thirty-three lochs north of the village and two lochs south of it. Day tickets cost around £4 and can be bought from Scourie Post Office.

→ **DIRECTIONS** – to find Scourie, you can take the A835 and then the A894 from Ullapool. Alternatively, take the A38 from Lairg. Once there, ask for local maps to the widely-flung lochs themselves.

⊨ **ACCOMMODATION** – you really cannot do better than the Scourie Hotel itself. It is geared heavily for anglers and a huge amount of information and advice is available. It's really an excellent fishing experience. Contact the hotel on 01971 502396.

TONGUE HILL LOCHS – HIGHLANDS

Tongue has a marvellous selection of lochs and some are quite easily accessible, especially as the terrain is not as wild as it is at Scourie, for example. Remember that these are popular during the height of the fishing season so it's a good idea, if you value peace and quiet, to take a good old tramp to the least accessible ones. Remember that, even though you're very far north indeed, the sun can be very powerful in such a clear, bright atmosphere. Take plenty of suncream and liquid refreshment – I'm thinking of water and not alcohol! And be warned the midges can be very bad, especially from May through to September on calm, warm days. A head net, as well as lotion, is recommended.

Don't let these things put you off, because the fishing can be quite magnificent. There's a mayfly hatch on a number of the lochs from June right through to early August, and do make a point of visiting Loch Hakel, which is one of the most beautiful lochs in the whole of Scotland.

Mostly, the trout average half a pound or so, but you will come across much bigger fish here and there, especially if you fish imitative patterns. Traditional wet and dry fly are all effective but black, red and brown seem to be the going colours. Once again, just because you're on a remote loch, don't expect the fish to be easy and ring the changes if things aren't working out for you. Also, approach the waters with caution because you will frequently find the fish close in.

There is also salmon fishing in Loch Naver and sea trout fishing in nearby Loch Hope. Both rivers at times have good runs of fish. Prior booking is generally essential.

SEASON – the brown trout fishing runs from 14 March to 7 October. For the salmon and sea trout fishing season, contact the Ben Loyal Hotel (see below)

TICKETS – a phone call to the Ben Loyal Hotel on 01847 611216 will reveal everything you need to know about the area. The hotel is also the headquarters of the Tongue and District Angling Association. Their keeper, Ian MacDonald, is available on 01847 756272. Also contact Altnaharra Hotel on 01549 411222 for the salmon fishing on Loch Naver and the sea trout fishing on Loch Hope. Some tickets are given to non-residents.

DIRECTIONS – from Lairg, take the A836 north to Tongue; it is approximately fifty miles. Once in Tongue, rely on local maps.

ACCOMMODATION – the Altnaharra Hotel and Ben Loyal Hotel are both geared up magnificently for fishermen. Ghillies, tackle shops and masses of advice. See above for contact numbers. Both highly recommended. There is also the Tongue Hotel, another favourite for anglers, on 01847 611206.

THE SHETLAND TROUT LOCHS

Of course, it's a long haul to get out to Shetland but once you're there, you'll never regret it, and you'll want to stay forever. I guarantee that there will be tears in your eyes as your ferry pulls away back to the mainland.

The appeal of Shetland is not hard to define: its loneliness, its beauty and lack of modern-day pace make it the perfect holiday destination. Unwind? You totally unravel! And then, of course, you've got the fishing itself, which can be quite wondrous. Okay, the magnificent sea-trout fishing of the past has declined but the brown trout fishing in over three hundred lochs is quite wonderful. And what variety of water you'll find – some are peaty lochans whereas others are alkaline and virtually transparent.

You won't find any mayfly out there but there is good feeding on shrimp, snail, olive and midge. Try any dry patterns, along with nymphs and traditional wet flies, and you'll probably do well. It also pays to listen hard to local knowledge. The Shetland Anglers Association have worked tirelessly to maintain the lochs on the islands as top-class wild-fishing venues and they publish a really detailed local guide book with immaculate instructions on how to find the hundreds of lochs. You can fish them all for a season ticket of £15! Even the boats are bookable at a weekly cost of £20.

If there is the explorer in you, I can guarantee that Shetland will offer the fly fishing holiday of a lifetime.

SEASON AND TICKETS – phone Graham Callender, the Honorary President of the Shetland Anglers Association, on 01806 503385. He will provide you with all the necessary information on tickets and seasons.

→ DIRECTIONS – P&O Scottish Ferries sail to Lerwick from Aberdeen. Phone 01224 572615 for ferry times and bookings. It is advisable to book in advance. The Shetland Islands Council on 01806 244234 also operates local ferry services for the area.

ACCOMMODATION – contact Shetland Island Tourism, Market Cross, Lerwick, Shetland ZE1 0LU on 01595 693434 for information on all kinds of accommodation.

HIGHLY RECOMMENDED FISHERIES

- Raith Lake, Kirkcaldy. Contact on 01592 646466. Very attractive. Rainbows into double figures, browns, brooks and goldens. Boats.
- Kingennie Fishings, Nr. Dundee. Call 01382 350777 for details. A truly beautiful big fish water. An exciting challenge. Highly recommended.
- Newton Farm, Nr. Dundee. Phone 01382 542513. Attractive, shallow, five-acre water. Big fish, top water feeding. Excellent.
- Moffat Fishery, Dumfries and Galloway. Call 01683 221068. Crystal-clear fishing. Lovely conditioned fish, some brookies. Interesting fishing.
- Springwater Trout Fishery, Nr. Ayr, East Ayrshire. Phone 01292 560343 for more information. Excellently run, with super fish. Great lodge.
- Haylie Fishery, Nr. Largs, North Ayrshire. Contact on 01475 676005. Beautifully scenic. Great view of Clyde estuary. Some big fish.
- Lawfield Fishery, Nr. Glasgow. Call 01505 874182. Great scenery. Very welcoming. Good quality fish. Well patronised by locals – a good sign.

FLY-FISHING SITES IN IRELAND

1. Lough Corrib
2. Lough Mask
3. Lough Carra
4. Lough Arrow
5. Lough Melvin
6. The Sperrins
7. Glenowen
8. Straid Trout Fishery
9. Lough Ennell
10. Aughrim Trout Fishery
11. Ballyvolane House & The River Blackwater
12. Lough Currane

> *It's sad but true that when many anglers from across the seas think of Ireland their thoughts concentrate on south of the border. Of course, there is superb fishing there but I urge you to reconsider what the north has to offer. In fact, my own belief is – and I've seen virtually every water in all of the island – that the north can offer every bit as much as the south. We've got some fabulous salmon runs, you can pick up sea trout in all manner of unexpected places and some of our brown trout fishing is beyond compare. What's more, most of it – or at least much of it – is one big, well-kept secret. Everybody knows about the big southern loughs, Mask, Corrib and Conn, but we've got waters that would make any southerner sit up!*

MIKE SHORT, IRISH WRITER, CELEBRITY AND ADVISOR
TO THE NORTHERN IRISH TOURIST BOARD

There you have it, Ireland – whether North or South of the border – is a place teeming with opportunities for the game fisherman. There's wild fishing beyond compare but, at the same time, there are the more intimate, commercial fisheries where you can build up your confidence! But then, Ireland is more than just about fishing alone. The countryside – so green, clean and uncluttered. The roads, often so empty you'd think yourself back in the 1930s. Sleepy villages. Welcoming bars, and, inevitably, a pint of Guinness waiting. In fact, most of the business is done in the bars. If you want to know anything, go into the bar, ask around and you will get to hear where there is a boat to hire, a ghilly willing to turn out or when you can expect the next hatch of sedges!

Improvements in ferries and air travel mean that Ireland is ever more accessible. You owe it to yourself to get out there and enjoy game fishing beyond compare.

LOUGH CORRIB – GALWAY

Corrib, in the west of Ireland, is truly a trout fisherman's paradise. It is over thirty miles long and covers some forty-four thousand acres, liberally scattered with islands and endowed with endless amounts of stunning fish! The lake varies greatly from one area to the next. In lower Corrib, for example, the water is generally quite shallow with depths averaging six to ten feet. The water here is very clear and weedy and there's an abundance of fly life. The northern end of the lake has many shallows too, but also has areas as deep as a hundred and fifty feet. These chasms are also of great interest to the fisherman as they hold brown trout in numbers, including ferox trout, some weighing in excess of fifteen pounds.

Corrib is a limestone lake and is rich in feeding. Trout are caught by fly fishermen as early as February, even in the shallows, with floating lines and teams of wet flies and nymphs. In March and April, local anglers wait eagerly for the Duck fly. This is a chironamid, black in colour with white wings, and it appears in weedy areas in great numbers. The trout gorge themselves, especially on the pupae. April can also be good with hatches of olives all over the lake. But the real attraction comes when the mayfly appears. From early May, right into June, this magical period sees many visitors on the Corrib as people flock here. Wet-fly fishing, dapped naturals and dry-fly fishing are all successful. The middle and top half of the lake fish best, particularly around Oughterhard and Greenfields. With a lull in July, August and September can fish well. Sedge patterns and wet flies take a large share of the catches.

Let's have a chat about the ferox... these fish are usually taken in the northern end of the lake and Inchagoill island is a famous area to try. They feed heavily on roach, small trout and char here. Trolled baits work well in the twenty- to thirty-foot band. However, be careful of bottom contours. Corrib, like all western loughs, can throw up reefs and shoals when you least expect them so be wary and never travel too fast over unfamiliar water.

☀ SEASON – the fly-fishing season opens on Corrib on 15 February and ends on 30 September.

⚡ TICKETS – The trout fishing is free on Corrib but a salmon licence is required. Many hotels issue licences. Alternatively, contact boatmen. Michael Ryan at River Lodge, Cong, County Mayo, on 00353 9246057, is very knowledgeable, and also rents out boats. Also try Michael Walsh, Ower Guesthouse, Greenfields, Headford, County Galway on 00353 9335446. The tackle shop in Clonbur on 00353 9246197 is a fund of information, too.

→ DIRECTIONS – Corrib, with its huge size, is really hard to miss. Situated just north of Galway, it is well served by roads both east and west.

▬ ACCOMMODATION – phone the Galway Tourist Information Office on 00353 91563081, or contact Basil Shiels at Ardnassillagh Lodge, Oughterhard, Co. Galway, on 091 552550.

LOUGH MASK – GALWAY

Lough Mask is a limestone lake of twenty-two thousand acres. Perch, eels, char, huge pike and probably some of the very best brown trout fishing in Europe. I will freely admit that possibly one of the very best months of my life was spent fishing Lough Mask back in 1991. I will have to admit that at the time I was primarily trolling for ferox trout: up until that date, I probably caught about a dozen or so in as many years of trying in Scotland. In that one month, I boated forty ferox trout between five and ten pounds.

Since then, I've been back principally with a fly rod, but the dream has continued. I just love Mask anyway. The softly enchanting west of Ireland. The villages and towns. The people. The lough islands where you can stop and brew a cup of heavenly tasting tea. The mountains in the mists. And the wonderful trout fishing. They say that the mayfly season between mid-May and mid-June cannot be bettered, but I've enjoyed exhilarating days with daddy longlegs and grasshopper patterns way into September. Yes, dapping is a very large part of what Mask is about and if you haven't tried it I urge you to get out with a boatman and learn this most satisfying of skills.

Of course, you can catch Lough Mask trout as you would on any Scottish loch or English reservoir, simply drifting, working teams of wet flies. This is blissful enough but, I repeat, do try the dap if you're anywhere near the west of Ireland between mid-May and the end of summer.

The beauty of Lough Mask trout deserves a special emphasis. These are absolutely pristine, wild brown trout, probably averaging around the one-and-a-half-pound mark. Certainly four- and five-pound fish are common. Talking about brown trout, Lough Carra, an offshoot of Mask, at four thousand acres a serious water in its own right, shallow and extremely fertile, produces browns that are probably the pick of a very exotic bunch.

Mask, especially as the sun goes down on a gentle-breezed day, is as close to magic as you can ever hope to come. I urge you to try it.

SEASON – early and late fly fishing in March and October can prove difficult and the very best of it really begins in May and runs through to mid-September.

PERMISSION – the fishing on Mask is free but it makes sense to join one of the local angling clubs for an outlay of £5 or so. Ballinrobe, Cong and Tourmakready all have their own associations, and they will help the visitor immensely with all manner of local knowledge and advice. They can also issue maps to show you the best access points.

BOAT HIRE – to get the very best out of Mask, you either need to take your own boat or hire one. Cushlough is a good centre for boat hire, as is the bay of Islands Park and Cahir Pier. On Carra, try Robert's Angling Service on 00353 9243046. Mr R. O'Grady of Ballinrobe on 00353 9241142 also has boats for hire.

DIRECTIONS – Lough Mask is situated off the N84, between Castlebar and Ballinrobe.

✉ ACCOMMODATION – all the towns around Mask have numerous small hotels and bed and breakfast facilities. Robert's Angling Service also operates a guesthouse for anglers. And try Ard Aoidhinn Angling Centre on 00353 9244009 and Derry Park Lodge Angling Centre on 00353 9244081. What's certain is that you will find warm hospitality around Mask from everyone you meet.

LOUGH ARROW – BRICKLIEVE MOUNTAINS – COUNTY SLIGO

Lough Arrow is uniquely beautiful. The Bricklieve Mountains rise to the west of the lake and as the sun sets, ancient burial mounds are silhouetted in this most lost and wondrous of Irish landscapes. This is definitely one of the unsung Irish heroes – over three thousand acres, spring-fed from under limestone streams. With no population or pollution to ruin its natural balance, the lough is home to wide-ranging fly hatch. Like many of the western loughs, Arrow is a haven for the mayfly: fish artificials or use real mayfly on a blow line. This is a time when the really big wild browns can be caught and some stunningly beautiful specimens are landed.

Buzzer fishing in May can be excellent while July and August see two large sedge hatches – the great red sedge and the green Peter sedge. The flies are really dense and often cloud round the boat like a mist. This provides great evening fishing and during the thirty minutes or so of the rise, the water can really look as though it's on the boil. By September, life is beginning to slow down and most of the locals go back on traditional wet flies.

There are many hotspots on this intriguing water. Look for areas around islands and reed beds. During the mayfly season, head for those areas of the shore that are tree-lined. Arrow is famous for its pristine, large browns. Two pounds is average, and threes and fours come out regularly, with the odd five-pounder thrown in. But how these fish fight! In the deep, crystal water these browns with majestic tails give any fisherman a time to remember.

☀ SEASON – trout fishing runs from April to October.
⚡ TICKETS – you cannot really do better for either tickets or boat hire than contacting Robert Maloney at Arrow Lodge, Kilmactranny, via Boyle, County Sligo, on 00353 7966298.
→ DIRECTIONS – Lough Arrow is in the north-west of Southern Ireland, just to the north of Boyle. Approach it on the N4 from the town.
✉ ACCOMMODATION – Robert and Stephanie Maloney run the aptly named Arrow Lodge right on the shores of the lough. I cannot recommend this too highly. The Lodge was built for fishermen nearly two centuries ago and rejoices in its current role. Comfortable, on the waterside and with the most knowledgeable of local ghillies, at the very least phone Robert for all the information you need on this fascinating water.

LOUGH MELVIN – LEITRIM/DONEGAL

Lough Melvin is a truly wonderful water, straddling the border between North and South, half in Leitrim, half in Donegal. A famous one for many reasons, in part because of its fish stocks. Lough Melvin has happy memories for me: I was a member of a party fishing there in March 2000 when Fred Buller, the famous fly fisherman and pike historian, caught one of the fabulously rare sonaghan trout for which Melvin is justifiably famous. This was an important moment: Buller had, by catching it, almost completed a full house! He'd caught all but one of every British freshwater fish species that swims... I believe the missing member is a vendace.

A sonaghan is recognisable by its colour, size, shoaling habits and huge tail. They average between three quarters of a pound and a pound and a quarter and they're dark in colour – a sort of gunmetal silver. That great big, distinctive tail means they fight frenetically, with extraordinary leaps. They tend to shoal down deep where they feed on daphnia. Small flies, therefore frequently pick them up and when you get one, you'll generally get others.

Then we come to another Melvin speciality – the gillaroos. Once again, these aren't huge fish, generally between a pound and a pound and a quarter, but what they lack in size is more than compensated for by staggering beauty. These fish are plastered with the most extraordinary, massive red spots. Catch them mainly in the shallows on dark flies on rough days. Gillaroos are primarily snail feeders and that's what they're looking for.

Melvin isn't done yet – brown trout, char, ferox trout, salmon and grilse... what a heady combination. Spring can be slow, but as soon as the weather warms, the lake comes alive. In early spring, most people are out trolling for salmon that come up the River Drowse. From April, the trout fishing really takes off. Late June onwards sees the mayfly hatch. As summer progresses, the grilse really begin to take over and you can catch those easily dapping with the mayfly. Look for the grilse, especially, around Laureen Bay and Rossinver Bay – two places much favoured by the locals. You can still troll and hope to pick up one of the ferox. These are magnificent beasts, not quite as large as those found in Mask and Corrib, but impressive nonetheless.

Do you go it alone or do you enjoy the company of one of Ireland's renowned ghillies? I would strongly recommend the latter. Melvin is a big water, does take some knowing and it pays you to look for some short cuts. Moreover, these men are invariably a delight – full of stories and full of tips.

SEASON – the salmon fishing opens on 1 February and the trout on 1 March. Fishing ends on 30 September.

TICKETS – at present there is no limit on the number of day tickets that are available at £10 per rod per day or £25 per rod per season. You can buy tickets from Sean Maguire at

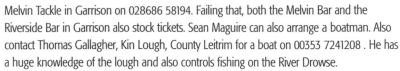

Melvin Tackle in Garrison on 028686 58194. Failing that, both the Melvin Bar and the Riverside Bar in Garrison also stock tickets. Sean Maguire can also arrange a boatman. Also contact Thomas Gallagher, Kin Lough, County Leitrim for a boat on 00353 7241208 . He has a huge knowledge of the lough and also controls fishing on the River Drowse.

➡ DIRECTIONS – Lough Melvin straddles the border a few miles south of Ballyshannon. Garrison is situated on the B52, at the south-eastern end of the water.

⊨ ACCOMMODATION – there is a huge amount of bed and breakfast and hotel accommodation locally. Mrs Flannagan at Lake View House offers an excellent bed and breakfast. Phone her on 028686 58444. Mr Ferguson, on 013656 58743, offers self-catering accommodation at Devenish Villa Holiday Homes. You can even camp at the Lough Melvin Holiday Centre for £6 a night! Phone 028686 58142 for details.

THE SPERRINS – ULSTER

I was absolutely knocked out by the Sperrins on a recent visit. This impressive mountain range stretches from Donegal in the west to Lough Neagh in the east, the heart and the hub of Ulster. The region's four main towns are Cookstown, Magherafelt, Omagh and Strabane. This is an area of outstanding natural beauty and, in many places, as lonely as any other area of Ireland. The three major species are salmon, brown trout and sea trout, although you might also come across the dollaghan, a unique species of Lough Neagh migratory brown trout. These run the many tributaries from mid July to the end of October. They average as much as two pounds and can grow to over six pounds. They travel a long way before spawning, in some ways rather like salmon and sea trout. Fascinating fish.

The Sperrins offer tremendous salmon opportunities, especially along the Foyle system. The main tributaries running through the Sperrin region from the Foyle are the Mourne, Derg and Strule. These are all fast flowing rocky rivers and salmon begin to enter them from April through to October. Then you've got the Owenkilleu and Glenelly rivers – classic spate rivers that fish very well in the summer and autumn. The Camowen and Owenreagh rivers also provide excellent backend fishing – often for grilse as well.

There are all sorts of surprises: to the north of the region, surrounded by mountains in the most awe-inspiring landscape, you'll find Moor Lough and Lough Ash – two waters both around thirty acres in extent and offering some classic wild brown trout fishing. On and on it goes – the Strule river, the Burn Dennet river... all marvellous waters, all set in stunning, wild countryside. Northern Ireland is increasingly offering a great deal to the visiting angler. There are tremendous possibilities across this beautiful country, but the Sperrins certainly are a jewel in a very considerable crown.

⛵ Season – the season in general runs from 1 April to 20 October.

🎣 Tickets – for the salmon fishing on the Foyle rivers, contact the Foyle Fisheries Commission, 8 Victoria Road, Londonderry, BT47 2AB, on 02871 34100. For fishing in the Lough Neagh system, contact the Fisheries Conservation Board, 1 Mahon Road, Portadown, Craigavon, County Armagh, BT62 3EE, on 02838 334666. For Loughs Moor and Ash, contact the Fisheries Conservation Board as above. David Campbell at the Tackle Shop, 28 Main Street, Newtownstewart, on 02881 661543 can provide tickets for the River Mourne, the River Strule and the Glenelly River. Also contact him for the Camowen River, the Drumragh River and the Owenragh River. Chism Fishing Tackle, 25 Old Market Place, Omagh, on 02882 244932, is also a fund of information.

➡ Directions – the Omagh Tourist Information Centre, 1 Market Street, Omagh BBT78 1EE on 02882 247831 will issue a detailed map of the Sperrins area.

🛏 Accommodation –contact the Omagh Tourist Information Centre as above. Strabane Tourist Information Centre on 02871 883735, Cookstown Tourist Information on 01648 766727 and Magherafelt Tourist Information on 02879 631510 will also give details.

GLENOWEN – LONDONDERRY

Glenowen is a brave project and a very necessary one too for Londonderry, Northern Ireland's second city. If you find yourself here as a resident or traveller, it means you don't have to go far to find some very pleasing fishing indeed. The fishery extends to something like nine or ten acres – a reservoir amidst twenty or so acres of public park situated close to the city's boundary. An unlikely place, but it is beautifully tended, attractive and gives you the feeling of being way out in the countryside. It's a government funded, co-operative exercise and one that obviously works very well. The water is clear, quite deep and the trout are in excellent condition.

You'll find some very friendly locals on the water, characters more than willing to give advice and perhaps lend a fly or two. Above all, what makes this such a heart-warming place, is the number of children that come here to learn. We all know that Ireland – north and south – is a wild fish paradise, but the fly-fishing can be difficult if conditions are against you. Hard for a child. Far better to work up his or her enthusiasm on a water like this. An attractive, safe, accessible water where fish aren't impossible to catch.

There are some good fish present – the fishery record is well into double figures – and they come to all manner of flies. In the deep water, however, it's not a bad idea to fish an intermediate line with lures. Alternatively, use a long leader and go for an imitative pattern. The fish will come up to the surface, so do have a selection of buzzers and dries along with you.

In short, it's great place to stop off if you're visiting. The family can be busy in Londonderry – increasingly a thriving city – or roaming the very attractive parkland, while you get a bit of peace and quiet.

SEASON – open all year.

TICKETS – contact Glenowen Fishery, Westway, The Rath, Creggan Estate, Derry City on 02871 371544. A three-fish limit plus catch and release is £11. A five-fish limit plus catch and release is £16. Junior tickets cost £6 and allow two fish to be taken.

DIRECTIONS – you need to get onto the west side of the city. Turn left off the Craigavon Bridge and turn right at the next mini-roundabout, which will be signposted for Carmelite Fathers. After about a hundred yards, turn left and go up a steep hill. Take the left at the T-junction by St Peter's School. After about a mile you will come to Creggan Country Park where you will find the fishery signposted. It is well known in the area.

ACCOMMODATION – contact Londonderry Tourist Information on 02871 267284.

STRAID TROUT FISHERY – COUNTY ANTRIM

Straid fishery, situated a few miles from Belfast, is a beautiful water, surrounded by fields and woodland. It's large, too, at twenty-two acres, and well stocked with rainbows. Average depth is between six and a half and seven feet, with occasional pockets going down to twelve. Water visibility is generally very good, it only really colours up after heavy rains.

Straid is popular for a number of reasons. Firstly, the size of the fish averages a healthy two pounds and they fight tremendously well. Secondly, stocking policies achieve just about the right balance. The water isn't too easy or too difficult, a perfect challenge for all. The ticket options also appeal; there's a whole range of different prices so anyone who just wants to come and fish for a couple of hours, including children, is well catered for.

All the usual methods work well and you'll find that the lake has a good sedge hatch with large numbers of buzzers, midges and olives. So the trout are well fed and used to looking for imitative patterns. Wet flies on an intermediate line prove a popular combination – try Green Peter, Silver Invicta or Hare's Ear. Buzzers are particularly effective throughout the summer, fished deep or in the surface film. Imitative patterns – shrimps, beetles and so on – can be fished on a floating line on a long leader, and watch for very careful takes.

SEASON – open all year round.

TICKETS – contact Straid Trout Fishery, Ballymure, Nr. Ballyclare, County Antrim, on 02893 340099. There is a whole range of ticket options available. For example, catch and release tickets cost £10, and the two-fish bag limit at £14 is very popular. A five-fish limit costs £20 and junior tickets are also available from as little as £6. Boats are also available at a modest cost and tuition is also offered.

→ **DIRECTIONS** – take the M2 north from Belfast and turn off at junction 4, signposted towards Larne. Travel through to the village of Ballymure and take the second right, signposted Straid.

⊨ **ACCOMMODATION** – contact the Belfast Tourist Information Centre on 02890 246609.

LOUGH ENNELL – CO. WESTMEATH

Lough Ennell is a fabulous water, no more than an hour's drive from Dublin itself. It's famous for holding the Irish record trout, way back in 1884, weighing in at 26lb 2oz. Ennell isn't considered a huge lough by Irish standards – only six or seven miles long! It is a limestone lake, which makes for fabulous water quality. At times visibility is between ten and fifteen feet. Mind you, it hasn't always been as clear as this. The local Lough Ennell Trout Preservation Association has forced down pollution. Their focus has been on the feeder stream, where they've clamped down on the amount of agricultural waste, sewage in particular, that has flowed into the lough.

It's got to be said that Lough Ennell isn't an easy water. Even experts – and a lot of them come out of Dublin – agree that a brace can be considered a good day. Mind you, remember that all the browns here are wild and there's no stocking whatsoever. Also, that brace of fish could easily be trout of between three and six pounds in weight. This is really very special fishing.

The early season can be slow. Then there come huge hatches of Duck fly. Some days fish will feed so heavily that they absolutely gorge themselves. Your own artificial really is little more than a needle in a haystack. Everything really takes off for the fly fisherman on or around the second week in May when the mayfly begin to appear. From mid May, therefore, to the end of the month, the fishing on Ennell is on full flow and this is when everyone wants to get afloat. The trout become catchable now, both during the day and in the evenings. Most locals would choose to go for a calm evening, just fishing a spent gnat as the light is beginning to go. Great stuff.

During the day, big dry flies work well – Wulffs, hackled mayflies and the local mosly may. Local lore has it that Pat Cleere ties the best flies for the loughs and his Green Peters really are something else.

After the mayfly come the sedge – Welshman's buttons – small and brown with yellow underbodies. These attract big fish, especially in the late evening.

Towards the end of the season, throughout August and September, the lake fishes best on dark, windy days. Try big wet flies then, bumbles and daddies and so on. Look for the shallows around Belvedere House, a rambling mansion close to the shore. Goose Island and Rinn Point are also places to concentrate on.

Ennell is a comparatively safe lake to fish on – especially compared with those monsters in the west. You won't find too many rocks so it's pretty safe to go out on your own, especially in calmer weather. Go and enjoy.

⚏ SEASON – the brown trout season on Ennell runs from 1 March to 12 October.

⚡ TICKETS – Lough Ennell is free fishing but please, please join the local Lough Ennell Trout Preservation Association. The Association charges a very modest annual fee and you can rest assured that all your money goes towards the preservation of the water and the promotion of the wild brown trout stocks. It's simply not fair to travel to Ireland, reap the harvest of other people's work and not put anything back in. You can join at any number of outposts in the area. You will need a boat to fish this water and the recommended contact here is Myles Hope, Lake View, Lynn, Mullingar, County Westmeath, Ireland.

➜ DIRECTIONS – the lough cannot be missed to the south of Mullingar, on the right-hand side of the N8.

⊨ ACCOMMODATION – contact the Irish Tourist Board in Mullingar on 00353 4448650 for information about accommodation in the area.

AUGHRIM TROUT FISHERY – WICKLOW

It's essential that I mention this extraordinary fishery, just south of Dublin. It's a four-acre lake set within a beautifully designed riverside park. The surroundings are quite gorgeous, but what makes it particularly important is the fact that it's designed for disabled anglers. The non-disabled are more than welcome, encouraged even, in the hope that they will help their disabled fishing companions around the lake. Pathways are designed to make sure that wheelchairs can get close to the water, yet are in no danger of capsizing. There's a lovely pavilion, good facilities and an exotic verandah where you can have a drink, sandwich and look out over the lake.

It's an ideal spot for any family touring the Wicklow area – there's a whole host of things to do and see in this beautiful part of Ireland and the fishing here can be very good. It's all about light line fishing really – certainly, go in the summer and you're unlikely to need anything more than a few buzzers and perhaps some Montanas. The fish fight well, are clearly visible and so can be stalked. But above all, it's this added element, knowing that disabled anglers are well catered for on a beautiful water, that really warms the heart. It's good to know that EU funds are from time to time put to really good use. The staff here are very helpful and positive-minded. A great day out.

☼ Season – open all year.

Tickets – contact Angling for All, Aughrim, County Wicklow on 00353 40236552. Prices are very reasonable – for example five euros for two hours fishing, two-fish limit, then catch and release; nine euros for four hours fishing, two-fish limit, then catch and release; and twenty-seven euros for an all-day ticket with a three-fish limit, then catch and release.

→ Directions – leave Dublin on the N11 following the coast through Bray and Wicklow as far as Arklow. Turn right onto the R747 to Aughrim. Go through the village, take a left at the traffic lights and the fishery is a short way down on the left. It is well-signposted.

⊨ Accommodation – contact Res Ireland on 0800 66866866 for information.

BALLYVOLANE HOUSE – COUNTY CORK

I felt it essential to offer Ballyvolane to the angler visiting Ireland with his family. There are two lovely lakes in the grounds of this eighteenth-century mansion, both very well stocked, with rainbows going way above five pounds in weight. The two lakes are kept private, reserved for hotel residents, so you know you won't be fishing shoulder to shoulder.

There are quite a few such waters in Ireland, but there's something rather special about Ballyvolane. The accommodation is quite excellent and the beautifully kept gardens boast an aviary and a croquet lawn. There's also a little carp fishery planned, which will be ideal for children.

It's been voted Ireland's best bed and breakfast by the AA and the food is superb. Sandwiches can even be served down by the lakeside.

If you want to be a little bit more ambitious, the hotel can also arrange fishing on some six miles of the River Blackwater at a very reasonable cost. The house is situated in a wonderful area very close to Cork, in the valley of the River Bride – a tributary of the Blackwater and a very interesting sea trout river at certain times. You can fly Stansted to Shannon now very cheaply indeed and this makes venues such as Ballyvolane more than accessible, even for a long weekend. A day on the lakes, an evening after sea trout on the Bride and a day on the Blackwater... a heavenly combination.

Tickets – contact Jeremy and Merrie Green, Ballyvolane House, Castlelyons, County Cork, on 00353 2536349.

→ Directions – from Cork, take the N8 towards Fermoy. In a few miles you will come to the River Bride. Just before the village of Rathcormack, take the right turning and follow the signs to the house.

LOUGH CURRANE – CO. KERRY

This is a magical place, about three miles long, but perched right down in the south-west of Ireland in County Kerry, next to the delightful town of Waterville. There can't be a more beautiful place in the whole of Ireland, and what a magnificent area to take a holiday in. Dingle Bay is just to the north and Bantry Bay a little way to the south. Fantastic cliffs, beautiful bathing and countryside to die for. But let's look at the fishing...

If you look back on the Irish specimen fish lists over the years, you will see that when it comes to sea trout, no water dominates more than Currane. For years, there have been huge, specimen sea trout running into the lough – a water that is free. Yes, you've only got to pay for boat charges.

In the spring, most troll for good-sized salmon and very large sea trout. Then, it's a matter of tobies and rapalas. From May, you can start taking sea trout on the fly. Fish wet flies lough-style – Bumbles, Green Peters, Daddies and so on. You'll also pick up the occasional grilse in June and July.

You'll need a boat. These are for hire all around the shoreline, along with local ghillies. This is a very dangerous lake, with many locks, and, being so close to the south-west coast, a storm can blow up at any time. It's essential to take a ghilly, for the first day at least. All the ghillies know exactly what they're talking about, but the famous family down here are the O'Sullivans. Like so much of what goes on in Ireland, you'll make contact with one of the clan in any of the local bars. One tip: evening fishing can be especially productive, so try to make sure you can both be out until last knockings.

Currane is linked to the sea by a tiny river known locally as Butler's Fishery. The fishing is just for guests of the Butler Arms Hotel, but can be tremendously good, especially when grilse are running. Finally, if the water is really high, consider Lough Capal, a very small water situated just above Lough Currane itself and linked by streams. When the water is high, the very biggest sea trout run up into this tiny lough. Thrilling stuff.

☀ SEASON – for salmon, 17 January to 13 September; for sea trout, 1 March to 30 September.

✸ TICKETS – free fishing, but you will need a boat. These are widely available.

➔ DIRECTIONS – Currane is just to the south-west of Waterville, easily seen from the N70 road.

⊨ ACCOMMODATION – contact the Tourist Information office at Waterville, on 00353 6694 74646, which is open May to mid September.

IRELAND'S COASTLINE

This is really something for the adventurous angler, perhaps the man on holiday who is looking for something a bit different. You've got to realise that Ireland has an extraordinary number of bays, estuaries, inflowing streams, lagoons... you name it, everything is there for incoming shoals of sea trout, bass and mullet. Of course, I'm not saying that every estuary and river mouth has superb sea trout fishing. That would be nonsense, but a little exploration often throws up some extraordinary results.

You'll need to check that fishing is available, but if you ask at the nearest bar, you'll often get all the details you want. Sea trout run best in most parts of Ireland through June, July and August. Try to get out on a rising tide, especially if it coincides with the late evening or dusk. Flies? Well, up in Donegal and Sligo, locals fish Rogan's Gadget as, with its silver belly and olive back, it looks like a sand eel, the basis of the sea trout diet close inshore. Don't fish the flies slowly. Get them going near the surface. Often you'll see a bigger 'v' following your own fly. Try casting into the current and letting the flow speed the flies' retrieve. But do experiment. You'll find a different pattern is needed from one night, or even hour, to the next.

Keep on the move until you contact, or at least see, fish. If you see locals congregate, you can be pretty sure that they know a hotspot. You'll get good, honest advice and a warm welcome.

It's with real trepidation that I recommend fly-fishing for mullet! These can be infuriatingly difficult to catch, but there are so many of them in shallow Irish waters throughout the summer that they can provide a really thrilling alternative to trout and salmon. Again, this is very wild fishing and you need to ask the locals for a bit of advice. Ideally, you're looking for lagoons where you can wade with security, in water that's no more than a couple of feet deep. You'll find that mullet follow very skinny water, coming in at the beginning of the flow. Often you'll see them working, tails out of the water, muddying the bottom. Wade very carefully until you get to within casting distance and put down as light a line as you can. A floating line is all you'll need with any small, dark patterns – any spider imitation should be a good start. Try them on a size fourteen hook initially, but go up or down if you're not getting any response. A slow, careful retrieve generally works better, and be prepared for quite a sharp, snaggy take. And then fireworks!

Do, always, make sure that you are investigating safe areas. Check up with locals about tides and any potential dangers. Never take risks and always make sure that you stay absolutely within reach of land.

IRELAND

141

This is truly wild fishing and it's wild fishing that Ireland is about. There's no point talking about logistics here. Most of the fishing will be free and is at its best from May through to September. Nor is there any point talking about directions. If you're anywhere near the coast then the chances are that there will be areas to investigate. Good luck and good exploring.

❧ HIGHLY RECOMMENDED FISHERIES ❧

- *Delphi Fishery, Leenane, County Galway. Phone them on 00353 9542211. The Delphi estate lies in an unspoilt valley in western Connemara, ringed by spectacular mountains. The fishery itself is a chain of beautiful lakes linked by one of Ireland's prettiest rivers. There's a good spring run of salmon between February and May and late May sees the arrival of grilse. From late June, salmon are accompanied by shoals of sea trout. An absolutely magnificent fishery and very highly recommended.*
- *Rathbeggan Lakes, Dublin. Phone 00353 18240197 for details. Very close to the centre of Dublin. A new water offering very good fishing and many facilities, including secure parking. A brave venture.*
- *Springwater Fly Fishery, County Antrim, Northern Ireland. A very promising water. A lot of fish caught on lures.*
- *The Caragh Fishery, County Kerry. Call 00353 669760102. Offers superb river salmon fishing and excellent lough browns.*
- *The Blackwater, County Waterford. Contact the Blackwater Lodge fishery on 00353 5860235. Recommended accommodation and first-rate fishing.*

⌒Author's Acknowledgements

I must thank Carol Selwyn for her unflagging patience in the typing, checking and researching of this volume. Thank you to Daniela and Anne for checking fine detail.

Let me also thank Anne Vossbark and her ghillies down in Devon. She has always been such a helpful presence, offering such wise words for nigh on twenty years. Also in the South West, thank you to Robin Armstrong for all his advice on sea trout and his help through the vicissitudes of life!

When it comes to the Wessex rivers, let me thank Reel-screamer Row and the late Dermott Wilson for valuable introductions. Up here in East Anglia, can I thank a clutch of men dedicated to the furtherment of trout fishing and of the environment in general – Joe Reed, Peter Suckling, Michael Robins, Paul Seaman and Mike Smith.

I'd like to thank Bob Church for all his writings over the years and for his advice and generosity. Thanks also to Eric Marsh for some exquisite grayling fishing on the Cavendish Hotel's waters, and to Peter Smith, Charles Jardine and Bob James.

Thank you to Andy Nicholson for all his help on Cumbria and to Leslie Crawford for her assistance on a very stormy day up in Caithness. A wonderful lady. Thanks to Gordon Heath, Christopher and Maddie and the late and great Arthur Ogilsby.

In Ireland thank you to Mike Shortt, all at the Northern Irish Tourist Board, Charles Plunkett at the Bell Isle estate and, above all, to Richie Johnston. All have shown me great generosity and help in the writing of the Irish section. Thank you, too, Richie for such a long-term friendship. And thank you also to Robert and Stephanie Maloney for a memorable stay on Lough Arrow – never to be forgotten.